As one of the world's longest
and best-known tra
Thomas Cook are the exper

For more than 13
guidebooks have unlocked the secrets
of destinations around the world,
sharing with travellers a wealth of
experience and a passion for travel.

**Rely on Thomas Cook as your
travelling companion on your next trip
and benefit from our unique heritage.**

Thomas Cook **traveller** guides

SWEDEN
Zoe Ross

Written and updated by Zoe Ross
Original photography by Alex Kouprianoff

Published by Thomas Cook Publishing
A division of Thomas Cook Tour Operations Limited.
Company Registration no. 3772199 England
The Thomas Cook Business Park, Unit 9, Coningsby Road,
Peterborough PE3 8SB, United Kingdom
Email: books@thomascook.com, Tel: + 44 (0) 1733 416477
www.thomascookpublishing.com

Produced by Cambridge Publishing Management Limited
Burr Elm Court, Main Street, Caldecote CB23 7NU

ISBN: 978-1-84848-223-4

© 2006, 2008 Thomas Cook Publishing
This third edition © 2010
Text © Thomas Cook Publishing
Maps © Thomas Cook Publishing/PCGraphics (UK) Limited
Transport map © Communicarta Limited

Series Editor: Maisie Fitzpatrick
Production/DTP: Steven Collins

Printed and bound in Italy by Printer Trento

Cover photography © Gräfenhain Günter/4CR

Contents

Introduction

For the large majority of people a holiday to Sweden means a weekend or a week's break in the beautiful cities of Stockholm and Gothenburg. But Sweden has far more to offer than that. The vast landscape incorporates dense forests, wonderful island getaways, idyllic lakes and snow-capped mountains, and there is a satisfying appreciation of art and history.

Stockholm is one of the most elegant as well as vibrant capital cities in Europe, with world-class museums exploring everything from the Vikings to contemporary art, an archipelago of islands making for tranquil summer

A Viking monument

cruises, and a fast-growing reputation as a gastronomic destination. Gothenburg, on the west coast, conveys a strong sense of culture with a renowned opera house and concert hall, as well as wonderful parkland and one of the country's most popular amusement parks. An extremely popular tourist activity is a cruise along the Göta Canal, a man-made waterway linking two of Sweden's most important cities.

Southern Sweden is a summer haven of sandy beaches, inland lakes and waterways and flat rural landscapes ideal for walking and cycling, not to mention fascinating islands such as Gotland and Öland, which retain traditional fishing villages as well as intriguing archaeological sites dating back thousands of years.

Northern Sweden has year-round appeal. In winter skiers flock to the slopes while tourist initiatives, such as the Ice Hotel, offer something novel to anyone wanting a winter break.

In summer, the midnight sun sees partying the night away take on a whole new meaning, with virtually continuous daylight for several weeks between May and July. In addition, this is the place to meet and learn about the Samis, the ethnic inhabitants of Lapland, who have not only preserved their culture but are more than happy to share it with inquisitive visitors.

Lovers of wildlife have much to do in Sweden, with birdwatching in the south and elk safaris and husky sledging in the north topping the list. History buffs have an enormous canvas too, from Viking relics to lakeland Baroque castles and stately homes, and a wide variety of open-air museums that lovingly preserve life as it was in days gone by. These museums are an obsession with Scandinavians, setting them apart from their southern neighbours.

Swedes have a reputation for being outdoor people, and with a landscape like theirs, who can blame them? All manner of sporting activities, from fishing to snowboarding, sailing to mountaineering, are on offer. For outdoor types Sweden has to be one of the premier holiday destinations in the world.

And finally, for gourmands, Sweden has the finest reputation for cuisine in Scandinavia, with its world-renowned *smörgåsbord*, superb fish and seafood and innovative dishes featuring reindeer and elk meat.

Introduction

View of Stockholm from Djurgården

The land

Covering an area of 450,000sq km (173,746sq miles), Sweden sits at the heart of the Scandinavian region, bordered by Norway and Finland and narrowly separated from Denmark by the Baltic Sea. The landscape was shaped approximately 10,000 years ago at the end of the last Ice Age, and Sweden's numerous lakes and waterways are a direct result of the melted ice.

Mountains and lakes

Northern Sweden is the most mountainous region, with the highest peak being Kebnekaise at 2,111m (6,926ft). Within this landscape are innumerable streams and powerful waterfalls that today provide valuable hydroelectricity to large parts of the country. Unsurprisingly, this is also the country's prime skiing area. In the southern areas of Svealand and Götaland, the inland landscape is characterised by lakes, both large and small, with the largest being Lake Vänern at 5,655sq km (2,183 sq miles). The man-made Göta Canal flows east–west between Stockholm and Gothenburg.

The coastline

Sweden's coastline is an impressive 2,400km (1,491 miles) in length,

Lakeland scenery at Ramnas near Västerås

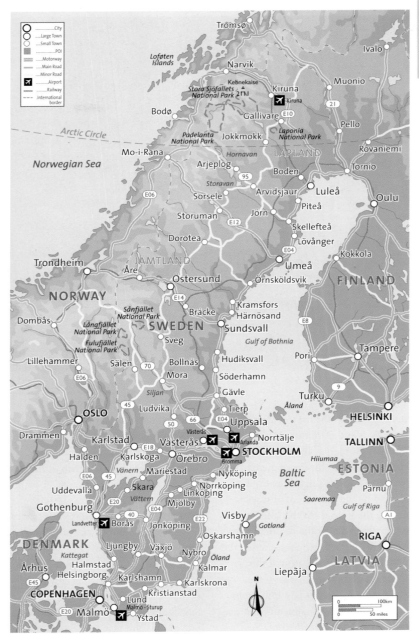

A distinctive red wooden house by a lake

stretching from the narrow strait between it and Denmark, and the northern borders with Finland. The smooth rocky archipelagos are one of Sweden's most distinctive features, formed by the movement of glaciers during the Ice Age. As the land level gradually rose over the centuries some of the islands became connected to the mainland, but sailing around the scattered islands is still one of the definitive experiences of a holiday in Sweden – both the mainland coast and the islands benefit from sandy beaches, making them popular summer destinations. In contrast, Sweden's western border is landlocked with Norway and follows the path of the Scandinavian mountain range.

The cities

Sweden's two main cities, the capital Stockholm and 'second city' Gothenburg, both evolved due to their harbour location, allowing easy trade with neighbouring countries. Stockholm is considered by many to be one of the most beautiful capitals in

Europe because of its island setting and waterfront views, while Gothenburg is often called the 'face of Sweden' for its outward-looking position facing the rest of Europe.

Geology

Sweden is rich in minerals such as iron, copper, lead and zinc, as well as silver and gold in some regions, and the mining of these ores underpinned the economy for many years. It has even contributed to the archetypal chocolate-box image of the country, when iron sulphate from a mine in Falu was added to paint to create the distinctive red colour that still adorns so many of Sweden's wooden buildings.

Climate

The climate of Sweden can be divided in two – north and south. In the north there are great extremes of temperature: between 20°C (68°F) in summer and −20°C (−4°F) in winter owing to its position within the Arctic Circle. There are also extremes of light and dark – in summer the polar day implies that the sun never sets below the horizon between mid-May and mid-July, while in winter the polar night results in several weeks when the area is plunged into darkness and the sun barely rises. Southern Sweden, in contrast, benefits from the Gulf Stream, giving the area a more constant and temperate climate, with summers averaging around 20°C (68°F) and

winters rarely below −3°C (27°F). Rainfall is highest in the west of the country, with Gothenburg claiming the title of wettest city. Snowfall is obviously heaviest in the north, but the whole country is likely to see some snow and ice each winter.

The natural environment

Approximately 60 per cent of Sweden is covered with forests: oak and beech in the south and firs and pines up north. Other trees that grow in abundance are ash, maple, linden and elm. This has given rise to an extremely important timber and paper industry that is a mainstay of the country's economy. The forests also provide shelter for a wide range of indigenous wildlife. Southern Sweden is also characterised by moorland, and the region is the prime agricultural area of the country. More than 2,000 plants are indigenous to Sweden, including a number of orchid species, and spring sees an explosion of colour across the country as the blooms emerge from the winter snows. Sweden's pride in its natural landscape is evident in it having been the first European nation to establish national parks in 1909: today there are a total of 28. In addition, there are no trespassing laws on natural land, so the country can be enjoyed by one and all. The coastline is also abundant in marine life, with a prime fishing environment that has supported the country for centuries.

Wildlife

Sweden's wildlife is as varied as its landscape, with different indigenous species making their home in the diverse habitats that make up the country. The pride that Swedes take in their landscape also means that large areas are protected as national parks or reserves, reducing the risk of their wildlife becoming endangered. The government has also set up an Environmental Protection Agency which outlines specific objectives such as clean air and sustainable forestry, all of which aim to conserve not only the beauty of the landscape but also its animal and plant numbers.

Reindeer are common in southern Sweden

Coastal areas

Sweden's long coastline means that its marine life is abundant, from cod to haddock, mackerel to perch, among others. There are also crustaceans such as lobsters and crabs. Once hunting was banned, seal populations improved considerably and the coastal areas are now home to large numbers of harbour and grey seals. Watching them basking on the rocks is a highlight of any trip. The maritime birdlife includes a variety of gulls, guillemots, sea swallows, herons and sea eagles. On the island of Gotland, the Gotland pony (*see p107*) roams wild, while its habitat is protected to ensure grazing land.

Inland areas

The overriding image of Sweden is of dense pine forests, and these are the most exciting areas for variety of wildlife. The elk (moose) is the most predominant species in terms of population, which is why annual hunting of the animal is still permitted. Numbers are currently estimated at 250,000, increasing each autumn at breeding time. Unfortunately many die in traffic collisions every year, and their large size (weighing up to 500kg/1,102lb and reaching heights of 2m/6½ft) means they are a danger to drivers as well, hence road warnings in elk-populated areas. The forests are also home to lynx cats and brown bears. The latter are the largest predators in Sweden, although their small numbers ensure that they pose little threat. Wolves and wolverines are also present and are now protected under Swedish law. In the southern regions, roe deer are very much in force, as well as smaller populations of red and fallow deer. Foxes, hares and beavers are common sights. Birds of prey include buzzards and hawks, while other inland birdlife includes pheasants, nightingales and wagtails. Along the inland waterways, kingfishers are a beautiful sight, while the many lakes and streams are home to an abundance of salmon, trout and carp, making angling one of the most popular activities in Sweden.

Northern Sweden

The reindeers of the north may be Sweden's most iconic animals but they are now largely domesticated and kept by the Samis for their meat, skin and ability to pull sledges. Huskies, also domesticated, are a prevalent feature of life in the north. The population of musk ox is small and can be seen in the Härjedalen region. There is also a small population of polar foxes. Mountain birdlife includes grouse, ptarmigan and owls.

Sweden's forests are home to the brown bear

History

18,000 BC	Bronze Age begins.	**1317**	King Birger starves his brothers to death by locking them in the dungeon at Nyköping, but an ensuing revolt forces him to leave the country. In 1319 his three-year-old nephew is elected king.
12,000 BC	Reindeer herders settle on the land at the end of the last Ice Age.		
AD 800	Viking era begins with a settlement at Birka (*see pp112–13*). For the next 200 years the Viking warriors establish a tribal society and trading routes to Northern Europe and Great Britain.	**1344**	St Bridget establishes a convent at Vadstena (*see p72*).
		1349	The Black Death kills more than 30 per cent of the population.
1004	King Olof Skötkonung is baptised and brings Christianity to Sweden (*see p98*).		
1164	An archbishopric is established in Uppsala.		
1226	The Falu copper mine is opened, which produces the red-tinted paint so typical of Swedish buildings.		
1250	Stockholm becomes the capital.		
1275	Magnus Ladulås is pronounced King of Sweden.		

The 17th-century Swedish warship *Vasa*

1397   Queen Margarete establishes the Kalmar Union, uniting Sweden, Norway and Denmark under one sovereignty.

1434   The Engelbrekt revolt against taxes imposed by the Kalmar Union results in the Danish kings losing power in Sweden.

1477   Uppsala University is founded – the first in the country.

1520   King Christian II of Denmark executes 100 members of the nobility in Stockholm, in what is known as the Stockholm Bloodbath (*see p43*). In retaliation, Gustav Vasa establishes an army against Denmark.

1523   Gustav Vasa is elected King of Sweden on 6 June, which is now the country's National Day. Sweden leaves the Kalmar Union and Gustav Vasa restructures the economy, leading to the period commonly known as Sweden's 'Great Age'.

1527   The Reformation leads to Sweden adopting the Lutheran faith as its national religion and church property is confiscated.

1544   The Swedish monarchy becomes a hereditary system.

1568   Gustav's son King Erik XIV is imprisoned by his brothers, and Johan III is crowned king. Johan is also suspected of poisoning Erik nine years later.

1611   Gustav II Adolf is crowned king.

1626   Sweden becomes involved in the Thirty Years' War. Six years later Gustav II Adolf is killed in battle, and the throne goes to his six-year-old daughter Kristina.

1657   Denmark declares war on Sweden but King Karl X Gustav manages to lead his army across the frozen waters, known as the Great Belt, to Denmark and to victory.

1700   Denmark, Poland and Russia join forces in an

attempt to take over Sweden.

1742	Anders Celsius invents the thermometer.
1772	King Gustav III stages a *coup d'état* and restores absolute monarchy.
1778	Jews begin to arrive in Sweden after freedom of religion is declared.
1792	Gustav III is assassinated at a masked ball at the Opera House in Stockholm.
1809	A new constitution dividing power between the monarchy and the government results in Gustav IV Adolf being deposed. The Frenchman Jean-Baptiste Bernadotte, one of Napoleon's marshals, is chosen as the new king, and takes the name Karl XIV Johan.
1810	Construction of the Gota Canal begins, and is completed 22 years later.
1814	Sweden signs a peace treaty with Denmark and gains control of Norway.

1842	Compulsory education is introduced.
1855	Mass emigration to the United States begins (*see p92*).
1856	Sweden's first railway lines are established between Örebro and Ervalla, and Malmö and Lund.
1901	The Nobel Prize is established, as is compulsory national military service.
1905	Norway becomes independent of Sweden.
1912	Stockholm hosts the Olympic Games.
1917	King Gustav V hands over parliamentary control to the government, largely made up of Social Democrats.
1921	Women gain the right to vote.
1932	The Great Depression hits Sweden after a stock-market crash.
1936	The Welfare State is established.

1939	Sweden neutral during World War II.
1946	Sweden joins the United Nations.
1958	Women gain the right to be ordained as priests.
1961	The United Nations secretary general Dag Hammarskjöld, a Swede, is killed when his plane crashes. The warship *Vasa* is raised from the seabed (*see pp40–41*).
1973	Carl XVI Gustav is crowned king.
1974	The monarchy loses all political power and becomes purely ceremonial. ABBA wins the Eurovision Song Contest with their song 'Waterloo'.
1986	Prime minister Olof Palme is assassinated.
1994	Some 900 people drown when the *Estonia* sinks off the coast of Sweden.
1995	Sweden joins the European Union.
2000	The long-awaited Öresund Bridge opens between Sweden and Denmark (*see p81*).
2003	A referendum is held about introducing the euro in Sweden, but the people vote against it.
2007	Year-round celebrations held across the country for the 300th anniversary of Carl von Linné's birth.
2010	ABBAWORLD, a touring exhibition about Sweden's best-known pop group, tours Europe after plans for a museum in Stockholm were abandoned.

Guards at the Royal Palace, Stockholm

Gustavus II Adolphus (Adolf)

Gustav II Adolf (1594–1632) succeeded his father King Karl IX to the throne in 1611. Karl had greatly expanded Swedish territory in wars across the Baltic against Russia and Poland. Gustav Adolf inherited his father's imperial ambitions and pursued them with even greater military success.

Portrait of Gustav II Adolf by Jakob Elbfas (c.1630)

When he came to power, conflict was already brewing between the Holy Roman Empire and its Catholic allies and the Protestant kingdoms and princedoms of northern Europe. In 1618 this erupted into a long-drawn-out struggle known as the Thirty Years' War. Devoutly Protestant, Gustav Adolf's marriage to Maria Eleonora, daughter of the Elector (prince) of Brandenburg-Prussia, gave him a pretext to intervene in the conflict on the Protestant side, using the Prussian city of Elbing as his base of operations in Germany.

Bringing Sweden into the war at a critical period, when the Protestant alliance seemed close to defeat, Gustav Adolf inflicted a series of stunning reverses on the imperial forces. This earned him the soubriquet 'Lion of the North' from admirers in the Protestant countries of Europe.

As a general, Gustav led from the front, and was wounded numerous times, but as well as being physically brave he was also an innovative tactical genius, introducing light field guns which could be quickly moved to wherever they were needed most on the battlefield, and employing mobility in attack. History also shows him as a charismatic commander who was admired by his soldiers and officers. He also had the advantage of a strong and disciplined Swedish army, comprising battle-hardened troops and officers who had seen a generation of service in his father's wars against Poland and Russia.

Like a number of charismatic monarchs in history (including James III of Scotland, Peter the Great of Russia and Haroun al-Rashid, the Caliph of Baghdad), Gustav Adolf sometimes travelled incognito in his own realm and elsewhere in Europe, passing himself off as a common soldier called 'Captain Gars'.

His bravery – and short-sightedness – eventually led to his death at the Battle of Lutzen, when he charged by accident into the heart of an overwhelmingly powerful force of the enemy's troops.

The war dragged on for a further 16 years after his death. With the military and economic resources of both sides virtually exhausted, a peace treaty was signed in 1648. Gustav Adolf's body was eventually returned to Sweden, where it is interred in the Riddarholmskyrkan in Stockholm.

The throne passed to his young daughter Kristina, but his widow Maria Eleonora and the king's counsellors ruled as regents until she attained adulthood.

Statue of Gustav II Adolf

Gustav Adolf was much more than a mere warrior. Determined to build a modern kingdom, he founded Gothenburg and several smaller towns and cities, and also founded the University of Dorpat (Tartu) in Estonia, which was then part of Sweden's overseas empire.

Following his death, the Riksdag (Parliament) of Sweden decreed that he should be known in perpetuity as Gustav Adolf the Great (Gustav Adolf den Store), and he remains the only Swedish monarch to be so styled.

Politics

Sweden is a constitutional hereditary monarchy with a unicameral parliamentary government known as the Riksdag. King Carl XVI Gustav has been on the throne since 1973 as Head of State, but his duties are largely ceremonial, responsible for promoting Sweden both in his own country and abroad. Sweden's National Day is 6 June, which commemorates the day Gustav Vasa ascended the throne in 1523.

National government

The prime minister of Sweden (*statsminister*) is elected by a majority vote to serve a term of four years and heads a cabinet (*regeringen*) that runs ten ministries, and a parliament of 349 delegates. In addition, Sweden is divided into 21 counties led by a governor appointed by the cabinet. There are also the provinces of Norrland, Svealand and Götaland, although these divisions hold no political significance. There are elected ombudsmen who serve for four years and control the legal system.

DAG HAMMARSKJÖLD

Dag Hammarskjöld (1905–1961) was one of the most prominent Swedish politicians on the world stage during the 20th century, himself the son of a prime minister, Hjalmar Hammarskjöld. Having gained no less than four degrees at the University of Uppsala, Hammarskjöld entered public office after World War II and was highly instrumental in the establishment of the welfare state, as well as managing to keep Sweden out of NATO while keeping the country at the forefront of post-war economic reorganisation. Having served first as a delegate at the United Nations, in 1953, and then again in 1957, Hammarskjöld was elected the Secretary General of the organisation and oversaw almost a decade of great international strife. In 1956 he prevented Israel, France and Great Britain from using force against Egypt during the Suez Crisis, in 1958 he intervened in the war between Jordan and Lebanon, and in 1959 he mediated over problems in Cambodia, Thailand and Laos. He was, in large part, responsible for building the UN's reputation as a peacekeeping force to be reckoned with. The post-war period also saw the end of colonialism, and many of the newly independent nations struggled with their new-found status. One of the worst affected was the Congo, which, facing the prospect of civil war, asked the UN for help. Hammarskjöld spent a year trying to negotiate between different factions, but on 17 September 1961, on his way to meet the president of the Katanga province, his plane crashed and he and his fellow passengers died. The cause of the crash is not known, but many feel that there were political interventions. Hammarskjöld was posthumously awarded the Nobel Peace Prize.

The most prominent political party is the Social Democrat Workers' Party (SAP), which has been in power almost continually since the 1930s and is currently in power with a minority under prime minister Göran Persson. Other parties include the Moderate Assembly Party (MS), the Left Party (VP), the Christian Democratic Party (KDS), the Centre Party (CP), the Liberal People's Party (FP) and the environmental Greens (MPG).

The Swedish Constitution

The law of the land follows the Constitution drawn up in 1975, of which the primary condition is the people's right to freedom of expression, including the right to practise any religion freely, hold political demonstrations and have access to official documents. Another issue is the *Allemansrätten*, which literally means 'every man's right'. This allows any Swede to walk on, camp on and generally enjoy any land within the country, even if it is privately owned farmland, provided no damage is done.

The national flag

Local government

There is a total of 290 municipalities across Sweden, responsible for the handling of local transport issues, education and childcare, city planning and control, and cultural activities.

Sweden within the world

One of the most significant aspects of Sweden on the international stage has been its neutrality during times of war, including World War II. Because of its neutral status, Sweden is not a member of NATO. In large part this can be seen as a reaction to centuries of battle with its neighbours and a determination now to hold on to its independence. For this reason, too, Sweden was a late member of the European Union, only agreeing to join by a very narrow majority in 1994. It has, however, so far opted against using the euro. As a complement to its neutral politics, Sweden is also one of the foremost nations to participate in international peacekeeping operations.

The economy

Sweden's primary income comes from timber and iron exports. Car manufacturing has also been important. Sweden's renowned makes Volvo and Saab were sold in the 1990s to American companies, but in 2009 Swedish company Koenigsegg entered into negotiations to buy and hopefully resecure Saab's future. Fishing, telecommunications and pharmaceuticals are also important industries.

Culture

While the size of Sweden is comparable to that of France or Germany, its population figures are more in keeping with those of Belgium, making it one of the most sparsely populated countries in Europe. This has not prevented it from adopting a very tangible sense of national identity and Swedes hold fast to their cultural heritage, whether through the celebration of national dress and festivals, or an ongoing pride in their many artistic and scientific achievements.

The people

Sweden is a largely homogeneous society, and the archetypal image of tall, blonde and healthy people is very much in evidence all over the country. However, it has also had one of the most liberal policies on immigration and, particularly in the cities of Stockholm and Gothenburg, ethnic minorities are very much in evidence, although this is being far more regulated today than it has been in the past. Two native minorities are the Finns (approximately 30,000) who live on the border of their own country and owe their location to the period when Sweden and Finland were one nation, and the Sami (approximately 20,000), a population of reindeer herders who live in the north.

The most populated part of the country is in the south, along the Baltic Coast, although rural life is still very much part of the country's consciousness. Most Swedes who live in the major cities also possess a second home in the country to which they retreat in summer.

The Swedish language is almost identical to Norwegian and Danish, and residents of all three countries can understand each other without having to swap languages. As a nation, Swedes are generally considered to be formal and serious, placing a strong emphasis on good manners. However, they are also strongly egalitarian, dismissing class divides, and take pride in their liberal attitude towards taboo subjects like sex.

Dress

The national costume (*nationaldräkter*) was created at the turn of the 20th century, adapted from folk costumes from different parts of the country. For women, the blue skirt and the yellow apron adopt the colours of the Swedish flag, while the deep green and white are designed to emulate the forests and snow of the landscape. The stockings and laced up shoes are black. However, the official endorsement as national costume came only in 1983, when Queen Silvia wore it with pride on National Day. Men wear a red or blue waistcoat, with blue trousers.

The arts

Despite the language barrier, a number of creative geniuses have emerged from Sweden and made their mark on the international stage. In terms of literature, the greatest writer has to be August Strindberg, who made his name in both fiction and drama. Born into extreme poverty in 1849, Strindberg first tried his hand at acting but, failing in this, he turned to writing and found his first success with the play *The Outlaw* in 1871. Most of Strindberg's work fits into the naturalism and

expressionism movements, like that of his contemporary Norwegian neighbour Henrik Ibsen, and explores the theme of gender relations, concentrating on unhappy marriages and the clash of the sexes within the morally restrained world of the late 19th century. Strindberg himself married and divorced three times, so can be said to have had experience of the issues he addressed, although many critics have dismissed his work as misogynistic. His most famous work is the 1874 play *Miss Julie*, which continues to be staged all over the world to this day and was made into a film in 1999. With his last play, *The Ghost Sonata* in 1907, his use of expressionism (which was to become an important genre of the early

A Swedish Royal Navy band playing in the Kungsträdgården

A Carl Larsson illustration

20th century) earned him the title 'father of modern theatre'. Strindberg died in Stockholm in 1912.

Another successful writer who has had her work translated into several languages followed an entirely different path. Astrid Lindgren is known by children all over the world for her Pippi Longstocking stories, and various other characters, and many theme parks honour the writer and her creations across the country (*see pp81–2*).

Beloved by Swedes, but little known outside her own country, is Selma Lagerlöf (1858–1940). Her best-known work is *Gösta Berling's Saga*, published

ABBA

No one could have predicted the global phenomenon that would become ABBA in the 1970s, after they won the Eurovision Song Contest in 1974. Formed by two husband-and-wife teams, Björn Ulvaeus and Agnetha Fältskog and Benny Andersson and Anni-Frid Lyngstad in 1972 (their initials formed the group's name), their song 'Waterloo' shot them to international fame. Over the next few years they released hit after hit, including 'Money, Money, Money', 'Dancing Queen' and 'Mamma Mia', made a film and performed to packed stadiums in Europe and Australia. By 1983, however, the party was over – the songs were no longer striking a chord and, furthermore, both couples had divorced and the strain was beginning to show. The group split and never recorded together again. Benny and Björn went on to achieve success in theatre with their musical *Chess* in 1988, and *Mamma Mia!* (based on the group's songs) in 1999, renewing their popularity. Agnetha and Anni-Frid (Frida) attempted solo careers but eventually retired, and Agnetha became a recluse. The band weren't seen in public together until 2005 for the Stockholm premiere of *Mamma Mia!* Despite this sad demise, at the height of their success ABBA were Sweden's most successful export, even more so than Volvo cars, and their songs remain as popular as ever.

in 1891, as well as the children's book *The Wonderful Adventures of Nils* (1906). In 1909 Lagerlöf became the first woman to win the Nobel Prize for Literature.

The most popular and successful artist was Carl Larsson (1853–1919), whose frescoes adorn many of the country's most important buildings. He is best known, however, for his illustrations of his wife and eight children published in the book *Ett Hem* (*At Home*), which came to symbolise Swedish family life (*see p90 & p131*).

In music, Sweden has not achieved the international renown of composers from Norway and Finland such as Grieg and Sibelius, but it has produced world-class singers such as the soprano Jenny Lind (1820–87), known as the 'Swedish nightingale', and the tenor Jussi Björling (1911–60). Among pop musicians, apart from ABBA, The Cardigans, Robyn and José González have become international successes. In cinema, numerous Swedes have made their name internationally, both behind and in front of the camera (*see pp24–5*).

Sciences

In the field of science, Sweden has had more than its fair share of talent. Probably the best known is Alfred Nobel, who invented dynamite, among other things, and whose prize continues to honour scientific discovery (*see pp132–3*). The manner in which we refer to all living things is thanks to the meticulous cataloguing work of Carl von Linné, who simplified a previously arbitrary system into species (*see p125*). In his short life, Anders Celsius (1701–44), a professor of astronomy, not only proved that the *aurora borealis* (Northern Lights) phenomenon was the result of magnetic activity, but left a lasting mark on the world by inventing the Celsius thermometer, using 0 for the boiling point of water and 100 for the freezing point, although this was reversed after his death. Another short life was that of Carl Scheele (1742–86), but within that time he discovered a vast array of chemical compounds including chlorine, hydrogen fluoride and citric acid. Many mobile phone users around the world can thank Lars Magnus Ericsson (1846–1926) for their contraption. Ericsson began his career as a mechanic repairing telephone equipment but moved on to designing telephone systems, including the first telephone handsets, eventually creating a vast enterprise that is today one of Sweden's most important industries.

Statue of scientist Carl von Linné

Film stars and film-makers

Many European countries embraced the media of film during the 20th century in their own distinct ways, from France's film noir to Italy's large-scale Cinecittà, but Sweden is the one European country that has really made its mark on the international film stage.

Film-makers

The first two film-makers to make their name in Sweden were Mauritz Stiller (1883–1928) and Victor Sjöström (1879–1960), who took the classic novels of Selma Lagerlöf (*see p22 & p126*) and transformed them into silent film classics, including

The legendary Greta Garbo

Gösta Berling's Saga, which featured a young unknown actress named Greta Garbo. Both directors would move to Hollywood and contribute to the golden age of silent film, before rejecting the American studio system and returning home.

Sweden's most famous film-maker, however, emerged 20 years later in the figure of Ingmar Bergman (1918–2007). Born in Uppsala, Bergman remained true to his Swedish roots and never fully embraced Hollywood, but his films nevertheless achieved international acclaim for their intellectual and existential themes. Bergman favoured a select group of actors and actresses to perform in his works, including his one-time girlfriend, the Norwegian actress Liv Ullmann, and the dialogue was largely improvised. His works include *The Seventh Seal* (1957), *Persona* (1966) and *Fanny and Alexander* (1982). The last won four Academy Awards, including Best Foreign Film.

Another Swedish talent in recent years has been Lasse Hallström (b.1946). Hallström first made his name as the director of all the ABBA music videos. A few years later he was launched on to the international

A banner commemorating the legend

film stage with *My Life as a Dog* (1985), and to even greater acclaim with *The Cider House Rules* (1999), starring Michael Caine, and *The Shipping News* (2001) with Judi Dench and Kevin Spacey.

Film stars

The most famous film actress to emerge from Sweden had a rather inauspicious start as the plump Greta Gustafsson, but when she followed Mauritz Stiller to Hollywood in 1925 she was transformed into the legendary beauty Greta Garbo (1905–90). During the silent era she became one of the world's most famous stars with her smouldering, sensual looks. Among her films is *Flesh and the Devil* (1927). Garbo was also one of the few actresses to be able to

make the transition from silent films to sound, with audiences revelling in her exotic and mysterious Swedish accent. This mystery was further enhanced by her dislike of publicity, with her most famous one-liner being the misquoted "I want to be alone". Among her most famous films are *Camille* (1937) and *Ninotchka* (1939), both of which earned her Academy Award nominations. Garbo retired in the 1940s and lived the rest of her life as a recluse in New York, but remains one of the most recognisable faces in film.

Following not far behind Garbo in legendary status was the Stockholm-born Ingrid Bergman (1915–82). Making her Hollywood debut in *Intermezzo* in 1939, Bergman went on to star in one of the most iconic films of all time, *Casablanca* (1942), opposite Humphrey Bogart. Several successes followed, but in the early 1950s her life was dogged by scandal when she left her husband and child to marry the Italian film director Roberto Rossellini. She didn't return to Hollywood until 1956 when she won an Academy Award for her role in *Anastasia*.

Another Swedish actress to have achieved iconic status is Anita Ekberg (b.1931), a former Miss Sweden who will forever be remembered for her frolics in Rome's Trevi Fountain in Federico Fellini's classic *La Dolce Vita* (1960).

Festivals and events

You might think that events would be thin on the ground in winter in Sweden, but you would be wrong! The famous Stockholm film festival takes place in November, and Nobel Prizes are awarded in December. The summer months, with their long daylight hours, are packed with celebrations and festivals – there is something for everyone, from jazz concerts to fishing.

January
Kiruna Snow Festival – At the end of the month ice sculptors take part in the world's largest snow festival.

March
Vasaloppet Ski Race – Famous cross-country skiing race between Sälen and Mora, commemorating the route taken by Gustav Vasa (*see p128*). (3rd)
www.vasaloppet.se

April
Walpurgis Night – On the last night of the month, bonfires, singing and fireworks celebrate the advent of spring.

May
Tjejtrampet – Over the last weekend of the month this female-only 51km (32-mile) bicycle race sets off from Gärdet in central Stockholm.

June
National Day – Every year Sweden celebrates its National Day with a range of festivities. In Stockholm the royal family gets involved. (6th)

Stockholm Marathon – Begins and ends at the Stockholm Stadium. (9th)

Vätternrundan – In the middle of the month there's a 300km (186-mile) cycling race around Lake Vättern.

Midsommar – Midsummer's night celebrates the year's longest day with bonfires, festivities and a tree decorated with ribbons (*majstång*). (22nd–23rd)

Restaurant Days – Various food-related events such as cooking contests and a waiters' race take place annually in Kungsträdgården in Stockholm.
www.smakapastockholm.se

July
Gatufesten – Begun in 1988, one of the country's largest street festivals is still going strong in Sundsvall. Rock concerts that have included names such as Tom Jones and Status Quo are the main focus, but there are also kids' activities and food from all over the world.

Stånga Games – Traditional sports, such as tossing the caber, have been held annually since 1924 (*see p109*). (8th–11th)

Stockholm Jazz Festival – A week-long celebration of jazz and blues. (16th–23rd)

Kukkolaforsen Whitefish Festival – On the last weekend of the month the return of whitefish to the Torneälven River on the border with Finland is marked by much fishing and cooking.

Skoklosterspelen – Viking tournaments, dramas and markets are staged. (27th–31st)
www.skoklosterspelen.com

August

Stockholm Pride – At the beginning of August, the largest gay event in Scandinavia celebrates with concerts, films and club nights. (3rd–7th)

Gotland Chamber Music Festival – In the first week of the month, features classical musicians from all over the world.

Dalhalla Opera Festival – Classical opera, ballet and other events in the outdoor amphitheatre carved out of a limestone quarry (*see p131*). (3rd–13th)
www.dalhalla.se

Medieval Week – Jousting, mystery plays and pageants bring the Middle Ages back to life on the island of Gotland. (5th–12th)
www.medeltidsveckan.se

Folk Dance Festival, Visby – Dancers from around Europe converge to display their musical cultures. (14th–17th)

Malmö Festival – A week-long festival of music, drama and crafts, starting off with dinner in the town's main square. (19th–26th)
www.malmofestivalen.nu

September

Riddarfjärden Regatta – Old wooden boats compete just off Stockholm quay on the first weekend of the month.

Lidingöloppet – The largest cross-country running race in the world. There are also less competitive events for children. (25th–26th)
www.lidingoloppet.se

October

Wisby Day, Visby – On the first of the month, music, markets and other events mark the history of this World Heritage city in Gotland.

November

Stockholm International Film Festival One of the most popular film festivals in Europe, premiering international works. It takes place in the last week of the month.
www.filmfestivalen.se

December

Nobel Banquet – The king presents the Nobel Prize Awards in Stockholm. (10th)

Festival of Light – young girls dressed in white parade in honour of St Lucia and to mark the beginning of the Christmas season. (13th night)

Malmöhus Christmas Market – A highly popular Christmas market.

Impressions

Swedes are an extremely patriotic people, but that's not to say that they don't welcome visitors. Their devotion to their land and landscape means that they want to show it off, and what better way to do that than to encourage tourists from abroad? And it is a landscape that will delight any holidaymaker, with idyllic lakes and offshore islands in the south, and vast pine forests and snowy mountains in the north. For urbanites, Stockholm promises to be one of the most elegant and graceful cities in northern Europe.

How to behave

While generally sporting a friendly and welcoming demeanour, Swedes are also renowned for their formality, and good manners are the backbone of their society. The handshake is *de rigueur* for both social and business occasions, and polite queuing is practised and expected. Since 2005 smoking has been banned in all public places, including bars and clubs, and excessive alcohol consumption is generally frowned upon. It's also obligatory, when having drinks with friends, to raise one's glass, say '*skål*' (the equivalent to the British 'cheers') and then drink, before placing the glass back on the table. Imbibing before this ritual toast is considered the height of bad manners.

Crime and security

Sweden is one of the safest countries in the world and, in general, tourists are highly unlikely to find themselves in what might be considered crime-infested areas in cities such as Stockholm and Gothenburg. Nevertheless, general common sense should always be employed, such as hiding valuables when you park the car or placing them in hotel safes. Pickpockets may be at large during the lively and crowded summer festivals that take place throughout the country, so make sure wallets and purses are safely out of view.

What to see and do

Because of its vast size, covering some 450,000sq km (173,746sq miles), no one should attempt to see the whole country in one trip unless they have a great deal of time (and perseverance). Most first-time visitors restrict themselves to the cities of Stockholm or Gothenburg, which is no hardship given their enormous appeal and wealth of attractions. Both cities are ideal weekend destinations, while a longer two-city trip has the added benefit of taking in some of the beautiful sights along the Göta Canal (*see p68*). Southern Sweden is the prime tourist area of the country, with its lakeside castles, sandy beaches and an archipelago of islands offering tranquillity, clean fresh air, a temperate climate and charming fishing villages. Ski enthusiasts, however, flock to the north in winter.

When to go

Say the word Sweden to most people, and the image conjured up will be of snowy mountains and dense forests. In reality, summer in the south is generally warm without being sweltering, making it ideal for sunbathing and watersports holidays. Even northern Sweden has respectable temperatures in summer, with the added benefit of the 'midnight sun' phenomenon when daylight

continues until about 11pm. The west coast, however, tends to be afflicted by rainfall almost year-round. Frankly, Sweden should be a winter destination only for winter sports fans, or those who want to see the Northern Lights, as a large proportion of the tourist sights throughout the country close down or severely restrict their opening hours in low season.

Getting around

Public transport in Sweden is excellent, as it needs to be to tackle the vast distances involved. Domestic air travel is easy between the country's 47 airports and reasonably priced, as well as being the most convenient, if less scenic, option. The flight from south to north, for example, is under two hours. The train network is also extensive in

Waterfront buildings in Stockholm

The Tunnelbana – the convenient metro system in Stockholm

the south, including links with Denmark and Norway, while there are several long-distance services between south and north, which offer the opportunity to enjoy the changing face of the landscape. The Inlandsbanen line is one of the most popular routes in summer, travelling from Kristinehamn to Gällivare through picturesque forests and mountains. Once you're outside the main towns, however, buses are usually the only option. The long coastline, multitude of islands and inland lakes and waterways mean that boat travel is both common and efficient. Ferries to the main offshore islands of Öland and Gotland are also high-speed car ferries, as are those between Denmark, Finland and the Baltic states. The best way to get around the majority of Stockholm is on foot, but there is also an easy-to-use and extensive metro system known as the Tunnelbana (T-bana), as well as tram and bus services. In summer one of the most idyllic ways to see the city and the nearby archipelago is via the wide range of ferry services, many of which provide a tourist commentary en route.

Driving

The condition of Sweden's road network in most of the country is excellent, and road safety records are among the highest in Europe. Only in the north can conditions become poor, when snow and ice restrict access. An added bonus is that all motorways and routes are toll-free, apart from the Öresund Bridge between Sweden and Denmark, which is still paying off its construction cost (*see p81*). Cars drive on the right-hand side of the road, so all cars are left-hand drive. Exceeding the speed limits (*see p183*) and driving under the influence of alcohol are serious offences, with high fines for offenders. All passengers, including the driver, must wear seat belts. Road signs generally follow the standard European symbols, but distinctive to Sweden are those warning against the presence of wildlife, particularly elks whose large

build can cause a serious, if not fatal, accident if a collision occurs. Popular tourist routes are signposted with brown-and-white signs.

The language
While Swedes, Norwegians and Danes can all communicate with each other with ease, Swedes are aware that theirs is an isolated language and almost all have a very good command of English. However, as with travelling in any country, it's always polite to learn a few pleasantries such as 'please' and 'thank you' (*see p185*), if only to acknowledge that you are a visitor in a foreign country.

The Nordiska Museum on Djurgården

Stockholm

Stockholm is considered to be one of Europe's most beautiful capital cities, not least for its picturesque location, spread across an archipelago of 14 islands. The city is a lesson in contrasts, from its wonderfully preserved medieval quarter, Gamla Stan, to the most striking of contemporary design in its shops and restaurants. In addition, fascinating museums, lush parkland and tranquil waterways make for an unforgettable experience. See p187 *for a map of Stockholm's public transport system.*

CENTRAL STOCKHOLM
Dansmuseet (Dance Museum)

The culture of dance from around the world, and the manner in which music and theatre from different civilisations have integrated over the centuries, is at the heart of this museum. There's also a fascinating section concentrating solely on the 20th century, in which so many dance forms emerged and evolved, focusing on artists such as Isadora Duncan and Michael Jackson.

Also on display are breathtakingly intricate costumes from the world of ballet. Temporary exhibitions relating to individual themes are also held regularly.

Gustav Adolfs Torg 22. Tel: (46) 8 441 76 50. www.dansmuseet.se. Open: Mon–Fri 11am–4pm, Sat & Sun noon–4pm. Closed: Sept–May Mon.
Free admission.

Hallwylska Museet

Set within a former private aristocratic home, walking into this museum is like walking into a time machine, where the late 19th century is brought back to life with furniture, furnishings and mannequins in period dress. Among the collections are pewterware, Dutch artworks and textiles.

Hamngatan 4. Tel: (46) 8 402 30 99. Open: Tue–Fri 11.45am–4pm, Sat & Sun 11.30am–4pm.
Admission charge.

Historiska Museet
(Museum of National Antiquities)

The most popular exhibits here are those focusing on the Viking era, with

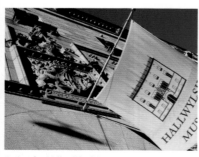

A sign for Hallwylska Museet

more than 4,000 artefacts. There are impressive medieval sections as well, including church art, textiles and Gothic sculptures, and a luscious Gold Room displaying jewellery and other precious items from various centuries. *Narvavägen 13–17. Tel: (46) 8 519 556 00. www.historiska.se. Open: May–Sept daily 10am–5pm; Oct–Apr Tue–Sun 11am–5pm except Thur 11am–8pm. Admission charge.*

Hovstallet (Royal Mews)

King Oskar II commissioned these royal stables in 1894 and the striking red-brick buildings were home to coach houses and a riding school as well as accommodation for the royal studs. Over the ensuing years, of course, the automobile began to take over as the primary means of transport, and the mews were then required to garage the royal Daimlers. Coaches and horses are still housed here for use on state occasions, including the stunning 'seven-glass coach'. Although it's still very much a working environment, visitors can view the area as part of a guided tour.

Väpnargatan 1. Tel: (46) 8 402 61 06. www.royalcourt.se. Tours: July–mid-Aug Mon–Fri 2pm; mid-Aug–Jun Sat & Sun 2pm. Admission charge.

Stockholm

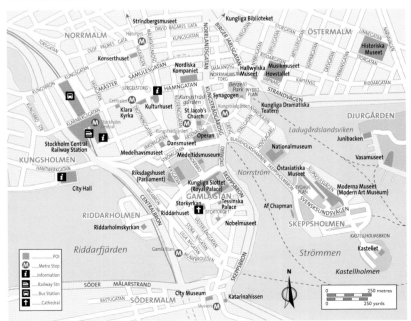

Kastellholmen

Jutting off the island of Skeppsholmen, the most prominent building on tiny Kastellholmen is the 1848-built citadel (Kastellet), even though its appearance is reminiscent of the medieval era. The island was once the city's naval base, and a naval flag is still raised every morning from the tower, while every weekday at noon a salute is fired from the cannons.

Closed to the public.

Klara Kyrka (St Clare's Church)

A convent stood on this site until the 16th century, when it was replaced by a church, which in turn was reconstructed after a fire in the 18th century. The most prominent feature of the exterior is the white spire, which dominates the surrounding skyline and was added in the 1880s.

Klarabergsgatan 37. Tel: (46) 8 723 30 31. Open: daily 10am–5pm. Free admission.

Konserthuset (Concert Hall)

Built in 1926, the city's concert hall is a mixture of neoclassical and Art Deco styles and has been home to the Swedish Royal Philharmonic Orchestra since its inauguration. The building is also well known for hosting the Nobel prizes every December. In the foyer are sculptures depicting figures from Greek mythology by Carl Milles, while in the main auditorium the 6,000-pipe organ is the finest in Sweden. Generally the building is only open for performances, but there are tours during the summer months.

Hötorget 8. Tel: (46) 8 506 677 88. www.konserthuset.se. Tours July–Aug daily 11am–5pm. Admission charge.

Kulturhuset (Cultural Centre)

Stockholm's cultural centre features exhibitions, live performances, and restaurants, and is generally the focus for all cultural activities in the

The citadel on Kastellholmen

city. Even the building itself, constructed in the 1970s with a striking glass façade, is the embodiment of the Modernist movement. Within the centre is the **City Theatre** (**Stadsteatern**), which opened in 1990 and largely stages contemporary works. *Sergels Torg 3. Tel: (46) 8 508 315 08. Open: Jun–Aug Tue–Fri 11am–6pm, Sat & Sun 11am–4pm; Sept–May Tue–Fri 11am–7pm, Sat &Sun 11am–5pm. Admission charge.*

The Royal Dramatic Theatre

Kungliga Biblioteket (Royal National Library)

Every book published in Sweden has a copy stored in the country's national library, as it has been since 1661. The library was originally housed within the Royal Palace, but moved to the current location in 1877 in a building specially constructed for the purpose. Among its most valuable items is the 13th-century *Codex Gigas* ('Devil's Bible') from Prague, which miraculously survived a fire in 1697, the oldest known book in the Swedish language, dating from around 1280. As well as books and ancient maps, the library archives posters from the 19th and 20th centuries, vinyl recordings and, more recently, digital and electronic publications. The library no longer operates a loaning system, but most of its items can be removed to the Reading Room within the building for perusal. *Humlegården. Tel: (46) 8 463 40 00. www.kb.se. Open: Mon–Thur 9am–6pm, Fri 9am–5pm, Sat 11am–3pm.*

Kungliga Dramatiska Teatern (Royal Dramatic Theatre)

Sweden's national theatre opened in 1908 appropriately with a work, *Master Olof*, by nationally revered playwright August Strindberg. It continues to stage classic productions of Strindberg and other playwrights, as well as contemporary and international works in its different auditoriums. The grand marble façade is in the *Jugendstil* style of the times, while the foyer has a beautiful ceiling fresco by Carl Larsson and two bronze statues depicting tragedy and comedy. *Nybroplan. Tel: (46) 8 665 61 00. Tours available: mid-Jun–mid-Aug Mon–Sat 3pm; mid-Aug–mid-May Sat 3pm. Free admission.*

Medelhavsmuseet (Museum of Mediterranean and Near East Antiquities)

Ancient Greece, Rome and Egypt are the focus of the collections here. Tombs, ceramics, weaponry and sculptures from Cyprus, Egyptian mummies, marble columns from Greece and Etruscan gold

The National Museum

Sibyllegatan 2. Tel: (46) 8 519 554 90.
www.musikmuseet.se. Open: Tue–Sun
noon–5pm. Admission charge.

Nationalmuseum

The country's largest and most
important art museum houses
approximately 16,000 works of art, by
masters such as Rembrandt, Renoir,
Degas and Swedish artists including
Anders Zorn. Although some works date
back to the Middle Ages, the majority of
paintings are from the period between
the 17th and 19th centuries. Don't miss
the late 19th-century frescoes by
Sweden's favourite artist Carl Larsson
which decorate the main staircase.

There are also important collections
of French Impressionists and Russian
religious icons. For those interested in
interior design, there is a section
exploring the evolution of furnishing
in the 20th century.
Södra Blasieholmshamnen.
Tel: (46) 8 519 543 00. www.
nationalmuseum.se. Open: Jun–July Tue
11am–8pm, Wed–Sun 11am–5pm;
Aug–May Tue & Thur 11am–8pm, Wed
& Fri–Sun 11am–5pm. Admission charge.

jewellery are among the highlights,
alongside the largest collection of
ancient Islamic art in Sweden.
Fredsgatan 2. Tel: (46) 8 519 550 50.
www.medelhavsmuseet.se.
Open: Thur 11.30am–8pm, Fri–Sun
noon–5pm. Admission charge.

Musikmuseet (Music Museum)

From the 17th century to the
international phenomenon that was
ABBA, all manner of Swedish music is
explored in this comprehensive
museum. There are more than 6,000
musical instruments from various eras,
and the opportunity to try one's hand
at playing many of them.

Strandvägen

The majestic buildings, fronted by lime
trees and a quay of expensive boats and
yachts, that line this elegant boulevard
were occupied by wealthy merchants in
the early 20th century, and it is still
considered the finest street in the city.
The best view is from across the water
in Djurgården.

Strindbergsmuseet (Strindberg Museum)

The final home of the great Swedish playwright has been preserved as it was at the time of his death in 1912. The three-roomed apartment includes his bedroom, a bright dining room furnished with busts of his contemporaries Goethe and Schiller, and his study, where his blotting pad, pens and paper can still be seen neatly laid out on the desk. Also part of the museum is Strindberg's library of more than 3,000 books, as well as telescopes through which he liked to study the stars.

Drottninggatan 85.
Tel: (46) 8 411 53 54.
www.strindbergsmuseet.se.
Open: Tue noon–7pm (until 4pm Nov–Feb), Wed–Sun noon–4pm.
Admission charge.

Synagogen

Stockholm's Great Synagogue serves the city's small Jewish community, most of whom are refugees who fled persecution, or descendants of the latter. Built in 1870, the synagogue can accommodate up to 900 worshippers, with men downstairs and women upstairs. Outside the building is a Holocaust memorial to the 8,500 victims whose relatives now live in Sweden.

Wahrendorffsgatan 3.
Tel: (46) 8 587 858 00.
Tours: July–mid-Sept Mon–Thur 10am, noon & 2pm, Fri 10am.
Admission charge.

DJURGÅRDEN
Aquaria

Stockholm's aquarium is divided into seven different areas re-creating diverse ecosystems, from a rainforest to a

A view of Strandvägen from Djurgården

Gröna Lund is a popular amusement park

mangrove swamp, a coral reef and even a sewer environment. Fish and reptiles native to each environment can be studied and observed. There's also an area dedicated to the Baltic Sea, complete with a salmon ladder.
Falkenbergsgatan 2. Tel: (46) 8 660 90 89. www.aquaria.se. Open: mid-Jun–mid-Aug daily 10am–6pm; mid-Aug–mid-Jun Tue–Sun 10am–4.30pm.

Gröna Lunds Tivoli

One of the most popular amusement parks in the country features the famous Power Tower, a free-fall ride of more than 80m (262ft) – not for the faint-hearted. There's also a roller coaster, a Haunted House, a Ferris wheel and various other attractions to thrill and entertain.

Lilla allmänna gränd 9. Tel: (46) 8 587 501 00. www.gronalund.com.
Open: May–mid-Sept, hours vary – check prior to visit. Admission charge.

Junibacken

Sweden's most popular children's author Astrid Lindgren (*see p82*) is celebrated at this themed attraction for children, where characters such as Pippi Longstocking and Emil are brought to life (*see also pp81–2*).
Galärvarsvägen. Tel: (46) 8 587 230 00.
Open: Jun & Aug daily 10am–5pm; July daily 9am–6pm; Sept–May Tue–Sun 10am–5pm. Admission charge.

Museifartygen (Museum Ships)

Two early 20th-century ships, the icebreaker *Sankt Erik* and the lightship *Finngrundet*, have now been preserved as museums. The *Sankt Erik* operated during the winter months to keep shipping traffic moving in the archipelago and around the coast despite frozen waters. The *Finngrundet* was moored at sea to warn other sea traffic with its beacon of any shallow banks of water. Today the ships can be explored in full, offering a fascinating insight into the shipping industry 100 years ago.

Galärvarvspiren. Tel: (46) 8 519 548 91. Open: Jun–Aug daily 11am–6pm. Admission charge.

Nordiska Museet (Museum of Cultural History)

Fashion, furnishings and traditional festivals are all part of the museum that explores Sweden's rich cultural heritage. There's also a large exhibition devoted to Sweden's best-known playwright August Strindberg (*see p37*), with several original manuscripts, including his most famous work *Miss Julie*. The museum shop is an ideal place for souvenirs that are more stylish and authentic than those found in regular souvenir shops.

Djurgårdsvägen 6–16. Tel: (46) 8 519 546 00. www.nordiskamuseet.se. Open: Jun–Aug daily 10am–5pm; Sept–May Mon–Fri 10am–4pm (until 8pm Wed), Sat & Sun 1–5pm. Admission charge.

Rosendals Slott (Rosendal Palace)

Original furnishings and textiles in the so-called Swedish Empire style are on display in this royal palace. Built in 1823, the palace served as a summer residence for the royal family, but in 1907 was turned into a museum to preserve the style of the building.

Rosendalsvägen. Tel: (46) 8 402 61 30. www.royalcourt.se. Open: Jun–Aug Tue–Sun noon–3pm. Admission charge.

Skansen Open-Air Museum

Scandinavia adores its open-air museums, but Stockholm's Skansen is the prototype, being the oldest of its kind in the world. It's easy to spend an entire day here, wandering around the historic houses that have been relocated here from all over the country, re-creating village squares and 19th-century cobbled streets. Various craft displays, such as pottery making and weaving, are performed in the traditional manner, as are bread and liquorice making, with freshly baked produce on sale to visitors. Traditional stores such as an ironmonger's and a pharmacy are decorated and stocked as they would have been in the 19th century. There is also a schoolhouse, farmsteads, church, and a manor house, all of which can be explored to find out how people lived and furnished their homes 100 years ago. The zoo area is very appealing, bringing together native Swedish animals, such as brown bears, elks and reindeer, in large enclosures. The children's zoo allows the little ones to get up close with lambs, chicks and other young, depending on the season.

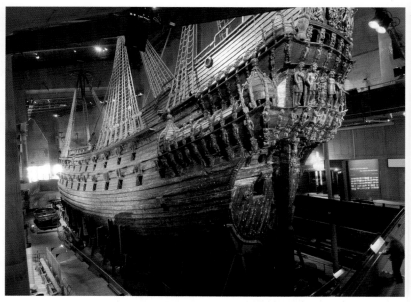

The *Vasa* is excellently preserved at the Vasa Museum

*Tel: (46) 8 442 80 00. www.skansen.se.
Open: May–Sept 11am–5pm; Oct–Apr
11am–3pm (longer opening hours for the
park and zoo).
Admission charge.*

Thielska Galleriet (Thiel Gallery)

This one-time private collection of
Nordic art, owned by a wealthy banker
named Ernest Thiel, is now accessible
to the public. Displayed in Thiel's
former Italian Renaissance-style home,
it includes works by such greats as
Edvard Munch, Anders Zorn and
Carl Larsson.
*Sjötullsbacken 8. Tel: (46) 8 662 58 84.
www.thielska-galleriet.se.
Open: Mon–Sat noon–4pm, Sun 1–4pm.
Admission charge.*

Vasamuseet (Vasa Museum)

One of the most spectacular museums
in the world, and Sweden's most
popular, it owes its reputation to an
exhibit of the fully preserved *Vasa*,
dating from 1628. The *Vasa* was built as
a warship during Sweden's battles with
Poland, but sank on her maiden voyage
just off Stockholm harbour, largely
because the gun-decks outweighed the
ballast at the base of the ship. The ship
was discovered in 1956 and brought to
the surface in 1961. She owes her
perfect condition to the muddy waters
that protected her for over 300 years.
Once the ship was brought on land,
25 skeletons, ceramics and various
personal memorabilia of the ill-fated
seamen were retrieved from her. Even

more spectacular is the exterior of the ship, intricately carved with biblical and mythological scenes, including a 3m (10ft) lion's head, all of which were intended to portray Sweden as a great warrior nation. Although most of these are a dull brown, originally they would have been painted in bright colours, and many are being restored to their original glory. Walking into the museum, where the ship takes centre stage, is a breathtaking experience, whether one is interested in maritime history or not. To get a fuller idea of the history of the *Vasa* and how she was restored, don't miss the short film at the beginning of the museum experience.

Galärvarvsvägen 14. Tel: (46) 8 519 548 00. www.vasamuseet.se. Open: Jun–Aug daily 8.30am–6pm; Sept–May daily 10am–5pm (until 8pm Wed). Admission charge.

Waldemarsudde

Prince Eugen (1865–1947) was not only a member of the royal family but also an acclaimed painter, and, at his request, his former home was turned into a museum after his death. At the museum, not only can you see wonderful landscapes by the prince himself as well as his studio, but also works by 19th- and 20th-century artists admired by the prince, such as Anders Zorn.

Prince Eugens Väg 6.
Tel: (46) 8 545 837 00.
www.waldemarsudde.se.
Open: Tue–Sun 11am–5pm
(until 8pm Thur). Admission charge.

GAMLA STAN
Kungliga Slottet

Although the Swedish royal family reside outside the capital at Drottningholm (*see p49*), Stockholm's Royal Palace is still the official residence, with all the royal administrative offices located here, and the venue for all state occasions. A royal residence has been sited here since the 13th century, in the form of a fortress, but it was in the mid-18th century, after Sweden's independence, that the palace

The grand exterior of Stockholm's Royal Palace

as we now see it was renovated in grand Baroque style. The royal apartments, the treasury and a museum of antiquities can now be seen as part of a guided tour. Note, however, that the apartments are closed to the public in September, when the king holds official state visits. The square in front of the palace is still the setting for the daily changing of the guard, which is one of the city's top tourist attractions.
Tel: (46) 8 402 61 30.
Open: mid-May–mid-Jun daily 10am–4pm; mid-Jun–Aug daily 10am–5pm; Sept–mid-May Tue–Sun noon–3pm. Admission charge.

Mårten Trotzigs Grand

A classic image of Stockholm is of its narrowest street, which measures only 90cm (3ft) in width and is still illuminated by lamplight.

Medeltidsmuseum (Museum of Medieval Stockholm)

In the 1970s building works for an underground car park changed into archaeological digs when large parts of the city's medieval foundations were uncovered. After the excavations a museum was built up around them, re-creating life as it would have been in the Middle Ages with workshops, stores and even a gallows.

Due to return to its original site at Norrbro in February 2010 after a temporary relocation to Sergelstorg, due to renovations of the bridge and the museum.

Tel: (46) 8 508 317 90.
www.medeltidsmuseet.stockholm.se.
Open: Tue–Fri 11am–7pm; Sat & Sun 11am–5pm. Admission charge.

Riddarholmskyrkan (Riddarholmen Church)

Dating from the 13th century, this is Stockholm's only surviving medieval abbey, although it has been renovated several times over the centuries (the spire dates from the 19th century). It is still the burial place for the royal family, as it has been for 700 years.
Riddarholmen. Tel: (46) 8 402 61 30.
Open: May & Sept daily 10am–4pm; Jun–Aug daily 10am–5pm.
Admission charge.

Riddarhuset (House of Nobility)

Considered one of the country's most beautiful buildings, completed in 1674, this was used by the Swedish nobility and at one time as the parliament building. The Session Hall is the most impressive part of the building, decorated with more

The streets of the Old Town

The main square of Stortorget

than 2,000 coats of arms belonging to the country's noble families.
Riddarhustorget 10.
Tel: (46) 8 723 39 90.
www.riddarhuset.se. Open: Mon–Fri 11.30am–12.30pm. Admission charge.

Storkyrkan (Great Church)

The oldest church in the city and the most important in the country dates from the 13th century. Its highlight is the Gothic wooden statue *St George and the Dragon*, created to commemorate Swedish victory over the Danes in 1471 at the Battle of Brunkeberg. Other features of note are the Baroque pulpit, the silver altar and the 600-year-old bronze candelabra.
Trängsund 1. Tel: (46) 8 723 30 16.
Open: May–Sept daily 9am–6pm;
Oct–Apr daily 9am–4pm.
Free admission.

Stortorget

The main square of Stockholm's Old Town has a gruesome history. It was

here that the Stockholm Bloodbath took place in 1520. The Danish king Christian II ordered the beheading of more than 80 Swedish noblemen and then displayed their decapitated heads in a pyramid at the square in a demonstration of power. Today, however, the atmosphere is altogether more tranquil. The square is a popular resting stop during a tour of the area, with cafés and restaurants set within beautiful gabled houses supplying pavement tables in the summer months.

Nobelmuseet (Nobel Museum)

Alfred Nobel, the Nobel Laureates and their achievements are all documented in this museum set within the former Stock Exchange, which is also the site of the Nobel committee's discussions and decisions each year for the recipient of the literature prize.
Stortorget 2. Tel: (46) 8 534 818 00.
www.nobelmuseet.se.
Open: mid-May–mid-Sept Mon &
Wed–Sun 10am–5pm, Tue 10am–8pm;

mid-Sept–mid-May Tue 11am–8pm,
Wed–Sun 11am–5pm.
Admission charge.

Tessinska Palatset (Tessinka Palace)

Designed in 1697 by one of Sweden's greatest architects, Nicodemus Tessin the Younger, who was also responsible for the Royal Palace, this is one of the city's finest buildings and was in part inspired by Versailles near Paris. Of particular note are the Baroque landscaped gardens. Today the palace is home to the Governor of Stockholm.
Slottsbacken 4.
Closed to the public.

Västerlånggatan

The main shopping street of Gamla Stan is usually chock-a-block with tourists swooping down on the souvenir shops lining the route, particularly when cruise ships dock and disperse their passengers for a few hours of frenzied sightseeing. If you're looking for plastic Viking helmets, painted Dalan horses or any other piece of Swedish kitsch, this is the place to come.

OUTER STOCKHOLM
Etnografiska Museet (Ethnographic Museum)

The thousands of artefacts gathered here from around the world relate the history of human culture across the five continents. Many of these were brought to Sweden by some of the country's intrepid explorers and missionaries in the 19th and 20th centuries. Highlights include a Native American totem pole, original travelogues, and an exploration into how our perceptions of native cultures have changed from prejudice to appreciation.
Djurgårdsbrunnsvägen 34. Tel: (46) 8 519 550 00. www.etnografiska.se.
Open: Mon–Fri 10am–5pm, Sat & Sun 11am–5pm. Free admission.

Fjällgatan

A combination of wood-timbered houses and pastel-coloured stone buildings, together with old-fashioned street lamps, have earned this street the reputation as the city's most beautiful. In addition, its hilltop location affords wonderful views of the city and the archipelago.

Globen (Globe Arena)

Love it or hate it, you can't miss the vast spherical Globe Stadium on the Stockholm skyline. The building was completed in 1989 and has seating for up to 16,000 people for events such as ice hockey, football and rock concerts.
Globentorget 2.
Tel: (46) 8 725 10 00. www.globearenas.se

Hagaparken

One of the city's most popular parks was commissioned by King Gustav Vasa in the 18th century. It contains a number of architectural features including a Roman-style tent originally built as stables, a Chinese pagoda, and a

pavilion named in honour of Gustav III. The Haga Slott is a royal residence, now used for state occasions.
Tel: (46) 8 402 61 30. Open: Jun–Aug Tue–Sun noon–3pm.

Fjärilshuset (Butterfly House)

A re-created rainforest setting features around 100 tropical birds and 400 butterflies. The temperature within the enclosure is kept at 25°C (77°F) to ensure that the animals survive in their native habitat. There are also tropical gardens, containing rubber plants and cacti, and a Japanese garden with koi carp pools.
Haga Norra. Tel: (46) 8 730 39 81. www.fjarilshuset.se.
Open: Apr–Sept Mon–Fri 10am–5pm, Sat & Sun 11am–6pm; Oct–Mar Mon–Fri 10am–4pm, Sat & Sun 11am–5pm. Admission charge.

Judiska Museet (Jewish Museum)

Various aspects relating to Jewish culture, from religious artefacts to traditional ways of life, are explored here. There's also a sobering exhibition examining the horrors of the Holocaust.
Hälsingegatan 2. Tel: (46) 8 31 01 43. www.judiska-museet.a.se.
Open: Sun–Fri noon–4pm. Admission charge.

Katarinahissen

If you've got a head for heights don't miss this 38m (125ft) lift ride above the waterfront for wonderful views of the city. There's also a restaurant at the top.

Katarina Kyrka

Stadsgården 6, Slussen. Tel: (46) 8 642 47 85. Open: mid-May–Aug daily 8am–10pm; Sept–mid-May daily 10am–6pm. Admission charge.

Katarina Kyrka (St Catherine's Church)

One of the most beautiful churches in the city is this copper-domed edifice dedicated to St Catherine. In 1990 the building was almost totally destroyed by fire and it took five years of work to restore it to its original glory, even employing 17th-century techniques to ensure complete authenticity.
Högbergsgatan 15.
Tel: (46) 8 743 68 00. Open: Mon–Fri 9am–noon. Free admission.

Långholmen

Despite being called the 'green island' of Stockholm, Långholmen's claim to fame is less salubrious, as home to the city's main prison for 250 years, which only closed in 1975. The prison is now a fascinating museum, with former cells decorated as they would have been in the 18th and 19th centuries and exhibitions detailing the conditions and treatment of the convicts and life of the guards. Possibly one of the city's most unusual and interesting museums.

Långsholmsmuren 20. Tel: (46) 8 720 85 00. Open: daily 11am–4pm. Admission charge.

Millesgården
(Milles Estate Museum)

The former home of Sweden's greatest sculptor Carl Milles is now a museum dedicated to his work and to preserving his studio and art collection. Milles and his wife Olga donated the grounds to the public in 1936 when they moved to the USA, and all of the décor dates from that era. The highlight, however, is the grounds, which are dotted with replicas of Milles' sculptures (most of the originals are in museums around the country), including the Venus fountain and the head of Poseidon. There's also an area known as 'Little Austria' named after Olga's birthplace, which contains a chapel that serves as

Sculptures in the grounds of Millesgården

the artists' burial place. Those interested in horticulture will also enjoy the beautifully arranged terraces, hedges, perennial flowers and trees designed by Sweden's greatest landscape gardener Emma Lundberg.

Herserudsvägen 32, Lidingö. Tel: (46) 8 446 75 80. www.millesgarden.se. Open: mid-May–Sept daily 11am–5pm; Oct–mid-May Tue–Sun noon–5pm. Admission charge.

Naturhistoriska Riksmuseet
(Swedish Museum of Natural History)

All streams of natural history, including botany, zoology and geology, and themes from around the world are represented here. Exhibits explore the polar regions and the tropics and the evolution of life on earth – both human and animal – and there's also an intriguing exhibition exploring the human body, and an area devoted entirely to the Swedish landscape. There's also an unmissable area devoted to global warming and its effects on the earth, now and in the future.

Frescativägen 40. Tel: (46) 8 519 540 00. www.nrm.se. Open: Tue–Fri 10am–7pm (until 8pm Thur), Sat & Sun 11am–7pm. Admission charge.

Observatoriemuseet
(Observatory Museum)

Sweden has had a long and successful reputation within the field of astronomy, and anyone interested in the science should not miss the opportunity to visit this museum devoted to the universe and stargazing. The building opened as an observatory in the 17th century at a time when many of the great discoveries were being made, including those of astronomer Pehr Wilhelm Wargentin, whose study has been preserved. There's plenty of old telescopes on display, as well as an exhibition researching meteorological history. *Drottningatan 120. Tel: (46) 8 545 483 90. www.observatoriet.kva.se. Open: Apr–mid-Jun & mid-Aug–Sept Sun noon–2pm; Oct–Mar Tue 6–9pm, Sun noon–2pm. Tours: Sun noon, 1pm & 2pm. Admission charge.*

Sjöhistoriska Museet (National Maritime Museum)

The entire seafaring heritage of Stockholm, from the Viking era to the present day, is explored at length in the city's maritime museum. Memorabilia on display includes ancient navigational instruments, ship figureheads and furnishings as well as a reconstructed cabin of an 18th-century schooner. Ship models and sketches, as well as naval uniforms and weaponry, complete the list of artefacts, while different exhibitions follow diverse themes such as merchant shipping, cruise liners, shipbuilding and wartime naval activities. Even the building takes on a maritime theme – when viewed from the air the museum has the shape of a ship's anchor.

Djurgårdsbrunnsvägen 24. Tel: (46) 8 519 549 00. www.sjohistoriska.se. Open: daily 10am–5pm. Admission charge.

Skogskyrkogården (Woodland Cemetery)

In the early 20th century Stockholm realised that it needed to expand its burial grounds beyond the city centre and launched a competition for an architect-designed area in which to lay its citizens to rest. The plan by the architects Erik Gunnar Asplund and Sigurd Lewerentz was chosen for its blend of functionality and nature, with wooden buildings surrounded by pine forests. In 1994, the design was considered important enough to be designated a UNESCO World Heritage Site. The Woodland Chapel was designed by Asplund, but decorated by Carl Milles, including his sculpture *The Angel of Death*, while the crematorium contains three chapels divided by gardens for privacy and a tranquil lily pond in front designed to symbolise the cycle of life and death. Among the famous Swedes buried here is the Hollywood star Greta Garbo (*see pp24–5*). *Arenavägen 41. Tel: (46) 8 508 301 00. Open: all year.*

Stadshuset (City Hall)

One of the most prominent buildings on the Stockholm waterfront is the tower of the red-brick city hall, built in the early 20th century but emulating the gracefulness of the Renaissance

style. This is particularly apparent in the Blue Hall (so-called because the architect originally intended to paint it blue), with its wonderful colonnaded arches. Equally spectacular are the gold-and-glass mosaics in the Golden Hall and the frescoes by Prince Eugen in the Gallery of the Prince. By contrast, the Council Chamber, where the city council meets each week, is designed to emulate a Viking longhouse.
Hantverkargatan 1. Tel: (46) 8 508 290 59. Tours in English: Jun–Aug daily 10am–3pm; Sept daily 10am–2pm; Oct–May daily 10am–noon. Admission charge.

Stockholms Stadsmuseum (Stockholm City Museum)

Everything you ever wanted to know about the history of the city can be found here, from the early Viking era, through the Gustavian glory days, the Industrial Revolution, to the present day. Slide shows illustrate the most important events in the city's history.
Ryssgården, Slussen. Tel: (46) 8 508 316 00. www.stadsmuseum.stockholm.se. Open: Tue–Sun 11am–5pm (until 8pm Thur). Free admission.

Tekniska Museet (Museum of Technology)

All manner of scientific discoveries and achievements are uncovered in the various exhibitions here, which will delight any inquisitive mind, young or old. There's an intriguing exhibit on robots, a Machine Hall that explores advances in transportation from the simple bicycle to the steam engine and aviation, the history of telecommunications including the advance in telephone design, and an extremely popular model railway.
Museivägen 7. Tel: (46) 8 450 56 00. www.tekniskamuseet.se. Open: Mon–Fri 10am–5pm (until 8pm Wed), Sat & Sun 11am–5pm. Admission charge.

Ulriksdal Slott (Ulriksdal Palace)

Ulriksdal's royal palace dates from the mid-17th century, but much of the interior furnishings are from the period when Prince Karl XV and his wife renovated the palace in the 18th century, as well as the famous 1920s living room used by King Gustav VI Adolf. Also on display at the palace is the coach Queen Christina used in 1669 for her coronation procession.

Drottningholm Palace

The orangery in the grounds of the palace is now a museum of sculpture.
Solna. Tel: (46) 8 402 61 30.
Open: Jun–Aug Tue–Sun noon–3pm.
Admission charge.

Vin och Sprithistoriska Museet (Historical Wine and Spirits Museum)

A unique museum dedicated to wine and spirits, with a particular emphasis on Scandinavian favourites such as vodka, *glögg* (mulled wine) and *punsch* (a sweet spirit). There's a re-created wine merchant's shop from the 19th century, a potato distillery and a rousing history of Swedish drinking songs.
Dalagatan 100. Tel: (46) 8 744 70 70.
www.vinosprithistoriska.se.
Open: Tue 10am–7pm, Wed–Fri 10am–4pm, Sat & Sun noon–4pm.
Admission charge.

STOCKHOLM ARCHIPELAGO
Drottningholm Palace

The private permanent residence of the Swedish royal family since 1981 was built in the 17th century, then expanded and renovated over 200 years. Guided tours of some of the rooms are possible, with highlights being the Baroque state bedchamber and the library. Surrounding the palace are French-style gardens decorated with bronze sculptures. Also in the grounds is a Chinese Pavilion built in 1753 when chinoiserie was the height of fashion in Europe. Chinese and Japanese art still adorns the rooms.

Tel: (46) 8 402 62 80.
www.royalcourt.se.
Open: May–Aug daily 10am–4.30pm;
Sept daily noon–3.30pm; Oct–Apr Sat &
Sun noon–3.30pm.
Admission charge.

Fjäderholmarna

Only 25 minutes from the city by boat, the island is best known for its aquarium that displays native fish of the archipelago. For fish lovers of a different kind, it's also an ideal lunch or dinner trip to sample the freshest catch at the many fish smokehouse restaurants. There's also a craft village here.

Kymmendö

This tiny island, occupied by only 15 people belonging to a family that has lived here for more than 200 years, was made famous by August Strindberg. The author and playwright spent many summers on the island. It gave him the inspiration for the novel *People of Hemsö*, which is about the lives of the island people. The cabin where he worked can still be visited.

Möja

In the early 18th century Russian invaders waged war in the archipelago, and on Möja, one of the larger islands, you can still see the old bread ovens they used for baking. Apart from that, it's just pleasant to soak up the atmosphere of the 19th-century farming villages, fishermen's cottages and harbours.

Sandhamn

Literally meaning 'sand island', Sandhamn is best known as a swimming, sailing and sunbathing destination with long beaches, such as Trouville. But there are also plenty of interesting sights dating from the 18th and 19th centuries. The Customs House is a charming yellow stone building dating from 1752, while the harbour area makes for a pleasant stroll with its labyrinthine alleyways.

Utö

One of the most distant of the archipelago islands, Utö has 200 permanent residents and is a popular tourist area for cycling, fishing and swimming in summer. Its landmark sight is the 200-year-old windmill facing the sea.

Saltsjön steamship

This historic steamship has been sailing between Stockholm and Utö since 1925 and has a wonderful age-old atmosphere with mahogany furnishings and brass fittings reminiscent of days gone by. The ship was renovated in the 1980s, and now gracefully plies the archipelago during summer weekends, past forested islands, waterfront mansions and through narrow straits. There's a bar and an acclaimed dining room. In the evening there are jazz cruises as well.
Tel: (46) 8 747 98 55. www.saltsjon.nu

Vaxholms Fästning (Vaxholm Fortress)

This coastal fortress was converted into a museum in 2003 uncovering Sweden's naval defence projects. Within the exhibitions are explorations of military life during World War II, a vault from which bombs were launched in the 19th century and a guardroom-cum-prison from the 18th century. Mannequins in period costume as well as authentic furnishings add to the atmosphere.
Tel: (46) 8 541 718 90.
www.vaxholmsfastning.se.
Open: Jun daily noon–4pm; July–Aug daily 11am–5pm. Admission charge.

Värmdö

This island is best known for the porcelain factory in the town of Gustavsberg that was established in 1825. There is now a museum dedicated to the industry where pieces past and present can be enjoyed and workers' houses can still be seen in the harbour area.

Vaxholm Fortress

Raoul Wallenberg

Born into a wealthy banking family in 1912, Raoul Wallenberg was to make his name not as a businessman but as an accidental humanitarian hero, rescuing Jews from their fate in Nazi Germany during World War II. Wallenberg first became concerned about the Nazi persecution of Jews during a stint in Palestine in the 1930s when he met people who had fled Hitler's increasingly fearsome regime. On his return to Sweden he became a business partner with a Hungarian Jew based in Stockholm, which led to regular trips to Budapest. In 1944, when Germany occupied Hungary and rumours of the concentration camps began to reach the rest of the world, neutral countries such as Sweden were given the right to issue temporary passports to Jews seeking to flee their inevitable fate. Wallenberg was selected by the World Refugee Board, and travelled to Budapest where, through a combination of diplomacy and bribery, he issued thousands of protective passports. He set up Swedish 'safe houses' as hiding places, adorned with the Swedish flag. He also stopped an intended massacre of a Jewish ghetto by forming an alliance with powerful police chiefs. No one knows the exact number of Jews that

Raoul Wallenberg

Wallenberg saved, but estimates are given between 30,000 and 100,000. In 1945 the Soviet Army claimed that Wallenberg had been captured and killed, although this has never been proved. Many believe he either perished or still suffers under Russian rule in prison, based on reports from former prisoners released in the 1950s and 1960s. Today Wallenberg is honoured with a tree at the Jewish memorial in Jerusalem, Yad Vashem, in the Avenue of the Righteous Among Nations, which commemorates gentiles who helped save members of the Jewish population during the war. A square in Stockholm is also named after him.

Walk: Kungsträdgården

This long promenade in the centre of the city is one of the most popular gathering spots and, in summer, concerts and street performances are held here. Food kiosks lay out tables and chairs for you to enjoy the surrounding greenery and sun. There are two statues honouring former kings Karl II and Karl III, and a pretty pond fountain in the centre.

The walk covers about 400m (440yds) and can be done in 1 hour.

Start at the north end of the gardens at Hamngatan, which is lined with the Nordiska Kompaniet department store and home to the city's main tourist office.

1 Nordiska Kompaniet (NK)

At the north end of Kungsträdgården is Stockholm's most famous and elegant department store. International designer labels can be found here and

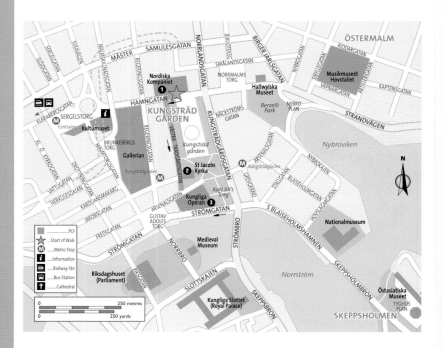

Nordiska Kompaniet *Hamngatan 18–20.*
Open: Mon–Fri 10am–7pm, Sat 10am–6pm,
Sun 10am–5pm.
St Jacobs Kyrka *Västra Trädgårdsgatan 2.*
Tel: (46) 8 723 30 38. Open: daily
11am–6.30pm. Free admission.
Services in English: Sun 6pm.
Kungliga Operan *Gustav Adolfs Torg.*
Tel: (46) 8 24 82 40. www.operan.se

the Swedish love of style is apparent in every display and item. The clock on the building's roof façade is one of the most recognisable symbols of the city. *Walk south along Västra Trädgårdsgatan to the bottom of the road.*

2 St Jacobs Kyrka (St James's Church)

Dating from 1643, and dedicated to the patron saint of pilgrims, the most striking aspect of the church is the beautifully carved wooden doors surrounded by exquisite stone-carved frames. Inside is the original baptismal font from the 17th century and an intricate gold altar.
Cross the road from the church to the Opera House.

3 Kungliga Operan (Royal Opera House)

At the end of the route is Sweden's Royal Opera House, dating from 1898. The most breathtaking part of the building is the Golden Foyer, a long, dazzling room lit by glass chandeliers and decorated with frescoes by Carl Larsson. The operatic programme generally consists of a good mix of classics, such as *Tosca* or *Die Fledermaus*, and contemporary works, as well as ballet performances.

The stunningly beautiful St Jacobs Kyrka

Walk: Skeppsholmen

Accessed via the Skeppsholmsbron (bridge), the island of Skeppsholmen makes for an ideal half a day's stroll. Along with its adjoining island of Kastellholmen, this was once the city's naval base, but today it is lined with lush gardens and a range of interesting museums and architectural features, such as the lovely octagonal design of the island's 19th-century church.

Allow about 3 hours to cover the whole island, including museum visits.

1 Af Chapman

The Swedish navy commandeered this former cargo ship, built in 1888, in the early 20th century as a training boat, but it was sold to the city of Stockholm after World War II and was converted into an innovative youth hostel in 1949.

Follow Västra Brobänken round to the left.

Af Chapman *Tel: (46) 8 463 22 66.*
Kungliga Konsthögskolan
Flaggmansgen 1. Tel: (46) 8 614 40 00.
Closed to the public.
Arkitekturmuseet *Exercisplan. Tel: (46) 8 587 270 14. www.arkitekturmuseet.se.*
Open: Tue 10am–8pm, Wed–Sun 10am–6pm. Free admission.
Moderna Museet *Tel: (46) 8 519 552 00. www.modernamuseet.se.*
Open: Tue 10am–8pm, Wed–Sun 10am–6pm. Admission charge.
Östasiatiska Museet *Tyghusplan 1. Tel: (46) 8 519 557 50. www.ostasiatiska.se.*
Open: Tue 11am–8pm, Wed–Sun 11am–5pm. Admission charge.

---

2 Kungliga Konsthögskolan (Royal College of Fine Arts)

Set within former naval barracks, students within this beautiful 18th-century building study painting, sculpture, architecture and even digital art, ending their courses with popular exhibitions open to the public.

With your back to the College of Fine Arts follow the left fork on to Svensksundsvägen, then turn left on to Exercisplan.

3 Arkitekturmuseet

Sweden has always been strong on design and aesthetics (*see pp90–91*) and here the history of architecture in Sweden through the ages is fully detailed, with models, sketches and photographs, as well as multimedia displays. Prominent architects themselves, and the history of their profession, are also highlighted.

On leaving the museum, turn left on to Slupskjulsvägen to the Modern Museum.

4 Moderna Museet (Modern Museum)

This is the best place in Stockholm to see contemporary art from the post-war era to the present day. Among the international masters on display within the collection of 5,000 works are paintings by Paul Klee, Picasso, Matisse and Dalí. In front of the museum are 16 brightly coloured sculptures, under the name *Paradise*, which were created in 1966 by the artists Jean Tinguely and Niki de Saint Phalie for a World Expo in Canada. Their creators donated them to the Moderna Museet in 1971, where they have been ever since. Behind the museum is a festival area, where many events are staged, such as the Jazz and Blues Festival every July (*see p27*).

Continue left on Slupskjulsvägen, turn left on to Brobanken, follow it left to see the Östasiatiska Museet.

5 Östasiatiska Museet (Museum of Far-Eastern Antiquities)

One of the finest collections of Chinese art in the world can be found here, including Buddha sculptures in a range of media and ritual positions, and ceramics from prehistoric times to the 20th century. Even the museum shop is decked out in the colours of the Orient, and sells a wide range of replica pieces, as well as authentic fans, clothes and jewellery from the region.

Return to Svenskundsvägen and turn right to return to the bridge and the mainland.

Walk: Skeppsholmen

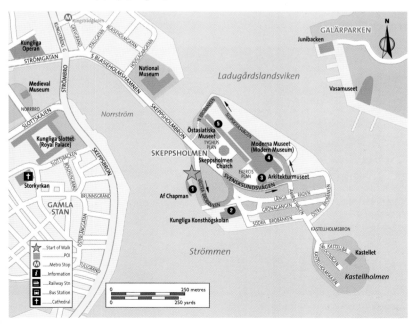

Gothenburg

Sweden's second city on the southwest coast is smaller and more manageable than Stockholm but is nevertheless a cultural hub with an abundance of museums, galleries and performance venues. The atmosphere is definitely cosmopolitan and many consider that the country's finest cuisine can be found here, particularly in the fish restaurants serving catches straight from the sea. The Old Town district has been beautifully preserved, and there are a number of parks for relaxation.

CENTRAL GOTHENBURG

Avenyn

Gothenburg's most fashionable street runs up from Götaplatsen and is lined with department stores, restaurants and bars housed in a collection of buildings dating from the 17th to the 19th centuries (*see p158*).

Barken Viking

Between 1909 and 1948 this large four-masted barque sailed between Sweden, South America and Australia carrying goods to and fro, including wheat and coal. In the 1950s it was decided to moor her permanently in Gothenburg's harbour, where

Statue of Poseidon on Götaplatsen

became a training centre
for novice sailors and ship catering.
Today the sailors' and captain's
cabins have been converted into hotel
rooms, all evocatively decorated
with maritime memorabilia, and
there's also a deck-top restaurant
in summer.
Gullbergskajen.
Tel: (46) 31 63 58 00.
Open: daily.

Carolus Dux and Carolus XI Rex

In the 17th century Gothenburg was
the most fortified city in the country,
due to its coastal situation and
proximity to Denmark. Remains of the
original bastions can be seen here.
Grönsakstorget. Closed to the public.

Christinae Church

Dating from the mid-18th century, the
42 bells of this church chime four times

Gothenburg

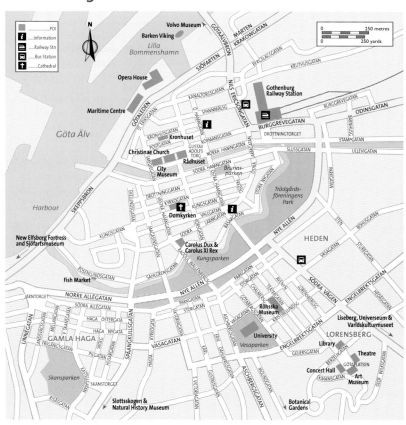

a day. It is often referred to as the German church because Sunday Mass is held in that language.

Norra Hamngatan.
Tel: (46) 31 731 61 92.
Open: Mon–Fri 11am–3pm.
Free admission.

Domkyrken (Cathedral)

Opened in 1815, Gothenburg's cathedral is in the neoclassical style displaying all the bright and clean lines so typical of Scandinavian design. The highlight is the gold altarpiece at the end of the nave.

Västra Hamngatan.
Tel: (46) 31 731 61 30. Open: Mon–Fri 8am–6pm, Sat 9am–4pm, Sun 10am–3pm. Free admission.

Domkyrken, Gothenburg's cathedral

THE SWEDISH EAST INDIA COMPANY

In the 18th century trade between Europe and Asia really took off and the Swedish version of the East India Company was founded in Gothenburg in 1731, the port city being an ideal trading post for silk, tea, porcelain and gems from the Far East. The Swedes were the fifth nation to set up such a company, after the British, Dutch, Danish and Portuguese, all of whom competed for the treasures available. In return for their Oriental imports, Sweden exported timber, iron and copper. The company, however, went bankrupt in the early 19th century. In 1985, the wreckage of one of the company's main ships – the *Götheborg* – was discovered. It eventually served as a prototype for a replica boat, the *East Indiaman*, which set sail in 2005 on an identical route to China, via Spain and South Africa, in commemoration of those early days of trade.

Feskekörka (Fish Market)

The building in which the city's famous fish market is held resembles the pitched roof and interior vaults of a church, hence the nickname 'fish church'. Piles of fresh fish and seafood from the day's catch are on display in this bustling market. There's also a café-cum-restaurant where you can sample the fish if you can't take your purchase home to cook.

Rosenlundsgatan. Open: Tue–Thur 9am–5pm, Fri 9am–6pm, Sat 10am–2pm.

Gamla Haga

Undoubtedly the most atmospheric part of the city, with cobblestone streets and wooden buildings, Gamla Haga was once

The fish market in Gothenburg

the working-class area of Gothenburg, made up of slum housing for workers during the Industrial Revolution. The area was renovated in the 1970s and is now a centre for craft shops and boutiques, but still retains something of its bohemian and offbeat feel.

Götaplatsen

Built for the World Exposition of 1923, this square is considered to be the cultural heart of the city, surrounded as it is by the concert hall, the city's main theatre and library, the art museum, and decorated with murals by Prince Eugen. In the centre of the square is a statue of *Poseidon* by the celebrated Swedish sculptor Carl Milles.

Göteborgs Konstmuseum (Gothenburg Art Museum)

The finest collection of Scandinavian art in the world includes works by Edvard Munch, Carl Larsson and Anders Zorn, as well as an important collection of Dutch, Flemish and 19th-century French works by the likes of Monet and Gauguin. Of local interest is the gallery devoted to the school known as the 'Gothenburg Colourists' of the 1930s and 1940s. The sculpture hall includes the classic onyx *Red Indian Head* by Carl Milles and *Family Group* by Henry Moore. The expansive ground floor of the museum is reserved for temporary exhibitions of contemporary art. *Tel: (46) 31 368 35 00. www.konstmuseum.goteborg.se. Open: Tue–Thur 11am–6pm (until 9pm Wed), Fri–Sun 11am–5pm. Admission charge.*

Göteborgs Maritima Centrum (Maritime Centre)

In the largest floating ship museum in the world, visitors can board the 1952 destroyer *Småland*, complete with its

Göteborgs Operan

original torpedoes, and the 1962 submarine *Nordkaparen*, to see what life was like for the sailors on board. In addition there are 16 other vessels, including steamships and tugboats, that complete the museum.
Packhuskajen 81–2.
Tel: (46) 31 10 59 50.
Open: Mar–Apr & Sept–Oct daily 10am–4pm; May–Aug daily 10am–6pm; Nov Sat & Sun 10am–4pm.
Admission charge.

Göteborgs Operan (Opera House)

With its waterside location, the spectacular setting of the city's opera house is matched only by its innovative design, emulating the harbour cranes and seagulls that constantly fly overhead. At 160m (525ft) in length and with the main stage encompassing

500sq m (5,382sq ft), this is not only Europe's newest opera house (1994) but also one of its largest. As well as classical operas, such as *Fidelio* and *Turandot,* and contemporary compositions, the stage is also used for ballet performances and Broadway musicals such as *Kiss Me Kate* and *Guys and Dolls.*
Christina Nilssons Gata.
Tel: (46) 31 13 13 00.

Göteborgs Stadsmuseum (Gothenburg City Museum)

Set within the former East India House built in the mid-18th century, the highlight here is the original Viking ship and an exploration of Viking voyages to the rest of Europe. The operations of the East India Company in the 18th and 19th centuries are also documented, as are many other cultural and archaeological aspects of Gothenburg's history.
Norra Hamngatan 12.
Tel: (46) 31 368 36 00.
www.stadsmuseum.goteborg.se.
Open: May–Aug daily 10am–5pm; Sept–Apr Tue–Sun 10am–5pm (until 8pm Wed). Admission charge.

Gustaf Adolfs Torg

Formerly known as Stora Torget, the city's main square is flanked by the City Hall (Rådhuset) and the Stock Exchange. The square is now named after the man who created the city and whose statue stands in the centre, Gustav II Adolphus, and celebrations still take place each year here on the anniversary of his death on 6 November.

Kronhuset

Gothenburg's oldest secular building, built in 1643, served as the Swedish parliament until 1660, when the four-year-old King Karl XI was proclaimed king, and then as a military warehouse. Today the building houses an exhibit detailing Sweden's so-called Age of Greatness between 1611 and 1721. The building is at its most popular during its annual Christmas market. Surrounding the building are 18th-century stable-like edifices in which craft stores and confectioners offer their wares.

Kronhusgatan. Tel: (46) 31 61 25 00. Open: by appointment only.

Liseberg

The largest amusement park in Scandinavia also features the biggest wooden roller coaster in the region, travelling at a speed of 90km/h (56mph).

In 2007 the hair-raising Uppswinget (Screaming Swine) opened. The ride makes a swing of 120 degrees, 40m (131ft) in the air at 80km/h (50mph). Other highlights include various white-knuckle rides, old-fashioned carousels and Ferris wheel, bumper-car rides, water chutes and rapids and a Viking boat ride. Also in the park is a performance stadium for concerts – everything from rock to classical – a

children's theatre, and various cafés and restaurants. The park is also open on certain days over the Christmas period – phone ahead for details.

Orgrytevägen. Tel: (46) 31 40 01 00. www.liseberg.com. Open: mid-Apr–end May Mon–Fri 3–10pm, Sat noon–11pm, Sun noon–8pm; Jun Mon–Thur 2–10pm, Fri–Sat noon–11pm, Sun noon–9pm; July–Aug Mon–Thur 11am–11pm, Fri–Sat 11am–midnight, Sun 11am–10pm; Sept–mid-Oct Thur–Fri 3–10pm, Sat 11am–10pm, Sun 11am–8pm. Closed: mid-Oct–mid-Apr. Admission charge.

Röhsska Museum (Design Museum)

As well as 18th-century Swedish textiles and furniture, both historic and contemporary, the permanent collections here include Chinese art dating back to 2000 BC and artefacts from ancient Greece and Rome. There's also an exhibit looking at the effects of the Industrial Revolution from its beginnings to the present day, seen purely through the eyes of design.

Vasagatan 37–39. Tel: (46) 31 368 33 50. www.designmuseum.se. Open: Tue noon–8pm, Wed–Fri noon–5pm, Sat & Sun 11am–5pm. Admission charge.

Trädgårdsföreningen

Within Gothenburg's most popular park is a palm house, built as a copy of London's ill-fated Crystal Palace in 1878, which features exotic plants

and a rose garden with more than 2,000 varieties of this classic bloom. There's also a herb garden and, in summer, the park is the setting for concerts and open-air theatre performances.
Tel: (46) 31 365 58 58. Open: Mar–Apr & Sept–Oct daily 7am–7.30pm; May–Aug daily 7am–9pm; Nov–Feb daily 7am–6pm.
Admission charge from May–Aug.

Universeum

This science and discovery centre includes a replica rainforest and an aquarium, a study of the universe and the planets and stars, an exploration of the workings of the human body, a history of inventions and robots, and a re-creation of Sweden's entire aquatic landscape featuring indigenous flora and fauna.
Södra Vägen 50. Tel: (46) 31 335 64 50.
www.universeum.se.
Open: July–Aug daily 9am–8pm; Sept–Jun daily 10am–6pm.
Admission charge.

Varldskulturmuseet (Museum of World Culture)

The city's newest museum is geared towards the understanding and coming together of all the world's cultures, challenging prejudices and celebrating differences. Among the permanent exhibitions are ethnographic objects from Latin America and other regions, and collections gathered during the years of European colonialism, while recent temporary exhibitions have focused on world music, the spread and prevention of AIDS, and indigenous tribes of South America.
Södra Vägen 54.
Tel: (46) 31 63 27 30.
www.varldskulturmuseet.se.
Open: Tue noon–5pm, Wed noon–9pm, Thur–Sun noon–5pm. Free admission.

AROUND GOTHENBURG
Botaniska Trädgården (Botanical Gardens)

The largest botanical gardens in the country are not to be missed for any avid botanist or horticulturist. Within the gardens are an arboretum, herb gardens, a Japanese garden complete with bridges and ponds, a rhododendron valley and greenhouses containing exotic plants including banana and a variety of orchids. The most popular area is the rock garden, which is divided into different climatic regions: the European area includes alpine plants such as edelweiss, the Asian area features plants of the Himalayas, while the Americas section includes snowdrops and yucca plants.
Carl Skottsbergs Gata 22A.
Tel: (46) 31 741 11 06. www.gotbot.se.
Open: daily 9am–sunset.
Free admission.

Harbour

Gothenburg's shipping industry may be past its glory days but the harbour, known as the 'port of Scandinavia', is still a bustling area of ferries and transport vessels. This is the place to come to take a trip around the Göta Älv, from which many of the city's waterside sights such as the Opera House and the *Viking* barque are best viewed.

Sjöfartsmuseum (Maritime Museum)

Exploring 400 years of Swedish maritime activity, from shipping to fishing. There's also an aquarium featuring indigenous Scandinavian species such as cod, hermit crabs and perch. Outside the museum is one of the most famous symbols of the city, the Mariner's Tower. It was erected to commemorate Swedish sailors who died in World War I, despite the country's neutral status, and depicts a

mother looking out to sea in search of her lost son.
Karl Johansgatan 1–3.
Tel: (46) 31 368 35 50.
www.sjofartsmuseum.goteborg.se. Open:
Tue–Sun 10am–5pm (until 8pm Wed).
Admission charge.

Slottsskogen

The city's most famous and popular park features an explosion of colour when azaleas and other flowers bloom in spring, but year round there is also a zoo, an aviary, walking paths and ponds. The park also has an observatory.
Tel: (46) 31 12 63 00. Open: daily during daylight hours. Free admission.

Trädgårdsföreningen is the city's most popular and picturesque park

Slottsskogen in its autumnal splendour

Göteborgs Naturhistoriska Museum (Natural History Museum)

Gothenburg's oldest museum contains a vast zoological collection examining natural life on earth. The first floor is dedicated to smaller earth and sea species such as crustaceans, reptiles and insects, but also here is the impressive 15m (49ft) stuffed blue whale, exhibited alongside its skeleton. The second floor concentrates on animals and birds, including a reconstructed dinosaur skeleton and a magnificent stuffed African elephant. There's also a section dedicated to five significant natural areas in Sweden, including Stora Karlsö (*see p107*) and Lapland (*see pp143–7*). *Linnéplatsen. Tel: (46) 31 775 24 00.*

www.gnm.se. Open: Tue–Sun 11am–5pm. Admission charge.

Nya Älvsborgs Fästning (New Elfsborg Fortress)

This 17th-century fortress on an island in the river features period dungeons, a former hospital and a church. Visitors get the most out of their visit by taking the dramatised guided tours, where costumed 'characters' such as a clergyman and a commandant relate 'their' lives in the complex 400 years ago. There are approximately ten tours a day. *Tel: (46) 31 15 81 51. www.stromma.se. Open: May–Aug daily. Admission charge.*

Volvo Museum

Gothenburg is the centre of the Volvo vehicle-manufacturing company (*see pp66–7*), and this museum explores the development of the quintessential Swedish car from its beginnings in 1927 to the present day. In addition to cars, the company produces buses, trucks and propeller engines, all represented here, besides exhibits detailing Volvo's participation in motor racing, and its world-renowned attention to safety and durability.

Götaverken, Arendal. Tel: (46) 31 66 48 14. Open: Jun–Aug Tue–Fri 10am–5pm, Sat & Sun 11am–4pm; Sept–May Tue–Fri noon–5pm, Sat & Sun 11am–4pm. Admission charge.

Whale's tail sculpture at the entrance to the Natural History Museum

The car's the star

Perhaps nowhere has Sweden's skill in and love of design (see pp90–91) been more visible over the decades than on the world's highways and byways, as it is home to two of the world's most influential car brands.

Volvo

The largest industrial company in Scandinavia began life in 1927 and has risen to become a global conglomerate, with manufacturing plants as far afield as Brazil, Australia, Thailand and the USA. As well as cars, the company also produces buses, trucks and racing vehicles.

The first car was the prototype ÖV4, created by the company's founders, Assar Gabrielsson and Gustaf Larson. Both wanted to design and manufacture a car that was sturdy enough to cope with the often difficult driving conditions on Sweden's roads. Their hands-on approach to the design of all the individual components was unique at the time, and came to be called the 'Volvo way'. From then on, the brand became synonymous with solidity and safety, and, in the 1970s, environmental friendliness. Every component is put through some of the most rigorous tests in the industry,

which has ensured the company's reputation for producing not only the longest-lasting cars, but also the safest. As early as the 1940s the cars were built within a strong frame that altered the impact of a collision from the body of the car to the front or rear ends. Volvo even invented the three-point seat belt that is now mandatory in every car in the world. In 1976 they also developed a catalytic converter that reduced fuel emissions harmful to the environment – all other manufacturers have now taken this up. Sadly for Sweden, the company was sold to the American Ford Motor Company in 1998, although Volvo still owns 50 per cent of its trademark and a vast majority of Swedes remain faithful to their national brand when choosing their latest car. A full history of the company can be explored at the Volvo Museum in Gothenburg (see p65).

Saab

While Volvo focused on safety design, Sweden's other car manufacturer, Saab, centred on the luxury segment of the market, seeing its competition to be brands such as BMW and Mercedes-Benz. The company, whose name is an acronym for Svenska Aeroplan Aktiebolaget (Swedish Aeroplane Ltd), began life manufacturing aircraft. They started producing cars in Trollhätten in the 1940s, and their sleek, streamlined design couldn't have been more different from the solid shape of the Volvo. All the early cars came in one colour only – green. It's thought that this was due to the abundance of paint they had left over after producing military aircraft in World War II. Among the innovations that Saab introduced to car design were headlamp wipers in 1970 and CFC-free air-conditioning in 1991. The company has also had great success with its rally vehicles, winning the Monte Carlo rally several times. In 1990 Saab was purchased in part by the American firm General Motors, but in 2009 the Swedish car manufacturer Koenigsegg negotiated acquiring the brand from its US owner.

An early Saab

Götaland

A land of swimming, sailing and fishing in forested lakelands and along idyllic canals, Götaland is the most popular tourist area in Sweden outside its two main cities. However, while much of the attraction of the area is the countryside, there are sophisticated cities like Malmö and Helsingborg to satisfy urbanites. To both the west and east of the region's coastline are tranquil archipelagos that come alive in summer for their excellent beaches and fresh seafood restaurants.

EASTERN GÖTALAND
Göta Canal

This man-made canal travels between Stockholm and Gothenburg along a beautiful landscape of birch forests and in summer three large passenger boats ply the route, allowing tourists to get on and off to visit sights along the way. The canal took 22 years to build in the early 19th century, and was largely constructed by soldiers to ease transport of goods between the two cities. Many of the ancient locks are still hand-operated by skilled and dedicated lock-keepers. It's also possible to rent your own boat for a more personalised trip, and rental companies will train the driver on how to navigate the locks before setting off. Motala is considered the capital of the canal region and there are various tours from here that explain the history of the canal. The canal's engineer, Baltzar von Platen, who died in 1830, two years before the canal's completion, is buried in town.

Kolmårdens Djurpark (Kolmården Safari Park)

This animal theme park is one of Sweden's most popular and successful attractions, particularly with children, who have the opportunity to get up close with tame animals such as goats and rabbits in the specially organised Children's Park. Three highlights are the Safari Drive, where you can navigate through the park in your own car

Kolmårdens Djurpark

through enclosures of lions, bears and wolves, the Marine World of penguins and seals, and the dolphinarium, where these beautiful and intelligent creatures enjoy performing tricks to a wonder-struck audience.

Kolmården. Tel: (46) 11 24 90 00. www.kolmarden.com. Open: May–Jun & Aug daily 10am–5pm; July daily 10am–6pm; Sept Sat & Sun 10am–5pm. Admission charge.

Linköping

Surrounded by undulating fields, the most prominent feature on the Linköping landscape is the spire of its cathedral, built in the 13th century. The town is one of the fastest growing in Sweden due to its expertise in the high-tech and IT industries. Nevertheless, it's an attractive place to visit, with parks and gardens, and a range of interesting museums to suit all tastes.

Domkyrkan (Cathedral)

One of the largest cathedrals in Scandinavia is also one of its best-preserved Gothic buildings. Highlights include a glass sculpture, a 16th-century altar and beautiful stained-glass windows. Next door to the cathedral is a museum documenting the history of the building as well as displaying textiles and silver items that were once housed in the church.

Tel: (46) 13 20 50 60. www.linkopingsdomkyrka.se. Open: daily 9am–6pm. Free admission. Museum: Borggården. Tel: (46) 13 12 23 80. Open: Tue–Sun noon–4pm. Admission charge.

Götaland

The Göta Canal

Linköping Domkyrkan is one of the largest cathedrals in Scandinavia

Flygvapenmuseum
(Swedish Air Force Museum)

Just outside the town centre, 50 military aircraft are on display in specially designed hangars, including a B17 reconnaissance bomber and a Spitfire. Following a major renovation in 2009, new features of the much-expanded museum include a science centre that explores all aspects of flight, and an exhibition dedicated to Sweden's role during the Cold War, including the remains of a Swedish plane shot down by the Soviet Union at the height of the hostilities.
Tel: (46) 13 28 35 67. www.sfhm.se.
Open: Jun–Aug daily 10am–5pm;
Sept–May Tue–Sun noon–4pm.
Free admission.

Gamla Linköping

Step back in time by wandering through the open-air museum which re-creates the town as it would have been 100 years ago. Houses, both aristocratic and working class, schools, shops and stables are all furnished in 19th-century style. Skilled craftsmen also produce traditional items such as the baskets and lace that are on sale in the museum shops.
Kryddbodtorget 1. Tel: (46) 13 12 11 10.
www.linkoping.se/gamlalinkoping.
Open: daily 10am–5pm.
Admission charge.

IT-ceum (Computer Museum)

Celebrating the town's importance to the Swedish computer industry, this

museum details the fascinating and incredibly fast rise of the computer that is now so central to our lives. Rather than a dull technical exhibition, however, it is very much the human aspect that is the main theme here, travelling from the beginnings of the technology to the present day and relating its effects on the way we live. There are also exhibits on computer games and their development, and the risks and results of the hacking culture. *Westmansgatan 45.*
Tel: (46) 13 28 65 24.
www.itceum.se.
Open: Tue–Sat 11am–3pm.
Admission charge.

Norrköping

Set on the Göta Canal, Norrköping's history is primarily industrial, but that does not mean its citizens are prepared to forgo beauty for business – the town is noted for its parks and, in summer,

an abundance of flowers. Nevertheless, the town that is often referred to as the 'Manchester of Sweden' has preserved many buildings from the Industrial Revolution era, such as cotton and wool mills, and these are well worth visiting. One of the old spinning mills is now also a museum dedicated to the industrial history of the town. Just outside the town are to be found more than 1,500 rock carvings, proving that the area has been inhabited for at least 2,000 years.

Omberg

On the banks of Lake Vättern and surrounded by woodland, the most important sight in Omberg is the Alvastra Abbey ruins. The original abbey was established in the 12th century, and was host to Sweden's patron saint Bridget and her visions, but it was deserted 400 years later. Also nearby is the Rökstenen, a 2.5m (8ft)

Exhibits at the Swedish Air Force Museum

Vadstena Castle

high rune stone inscribed with 800 symbols dating from the 9th century.

Sölvesborg

Sölvesborg dates back to the Middle Ages, when the area belonged to Denmark, and is now an attractive town of low-rise wooden buildings. The town was built up around a castle of the same name. The castle was destroyed by fire in 1564 and is now a ruin surrounded by a pretty park and is used as a backdrop for concert performances. In the centre of town is one of the few buildings to survive from the medieval period, the St Nicolai Kyrka (St Nicholas's Church), inside which are rune stones dating from the Viking period.

Vadstena

The most prominent building in Vadstena is the 14th-century abbey, but it is in the Klosterkyrka (Cloister Church) that the remains of the relics of the country's patron saint St Bridget are housed. There is also a convent of Bridgettine nuns here, and the town remains a centre of pilgrimage.

Also in town is the impressive Vadstena Castle, originally built as a defence fortress but converted during the Renaissance period.

Visingö

This island in the middle of Lake Vättern is the site of the country's first castle, the 16th-century Visingsborgs Slott, now a ruin. It was inhabited by the influential Brahe family and was adorned with artworks and sculptures, but after Count Per Brahe's death it was abandoned and fell into disrepair. In the 18th century it was inhabited by Russian prisoners of war who burned the castle to the ground on their departure. Today only the west wing can be seen, but it gives some idea of the immense proportions that the original must have incorporated.

The island is accessible daily by ferry from Gränna.

ÖLAND
Borgholm

The main town on this island, Borgholm comes alive in summer when yachts and other sailing craft crowd the harbour and tourists flock to the town to make use of the numerous fine beaches. The town is dominated by the vast ruined castle, where many areas, such as the Guard's Hall, a steakhouse and royal residential rooms, have been partially restored to show what life was like here over the centuries. The castle museum includes archaeological finds from the area, and models and exhibitions recreating life in the castle in its heyday.
Tel: (46) 485 123 33.
www.borgholmsslott.se.

Open: Apr and Sept daily 10am–4pm; May–Aug daily 10am–6pm. Admission charge.

Solliden

Just outside Borgholm, the summer residence of the Swedish royal family dates from the turn of the 20th century and is surrounded by beautiful landscaped gardens. Exhibits about the royal family are staged in summer in the pavilion.
Tel: (46) 485 153 56.
www.sollidensslott.se.
Open: mid-May–mid-Sept daily 11am–6pm. Admission charge.

Eketorps Borg (Eketorp Fort)

There are thought to be about 20 forts on the island of Öland, but Eketorp is the only one that has been fully excavated. Dating back to AD 400,

Boats moored at Borgholm harbour

the fort was uncovered in the 1960s, revealing a fortified farming village. During the Middle Ages the area was also used as a garrison. Today it is more or less an open-air museum with a theme-park atmosphere, with guides dressed in medieval costumes, theatrical performances and demonstrations of ancient crafts. The indoor museum, however, displays interesting items of jewellery and weaponry discovered during the archaeological dig.

Tel: (46) 485 66 20 00. www.eketorp.se. Open: May–Jun & mid–end Aug daily 11am–5pm; July–mid-Aug daily 10am–6pm; Sept Sat & Sun 10am–5pm. Admission charge.

Ölands Djurpark

This popular theme park includes amusement rides, a zoo with animals from all over the world, a dinosaur park, circus acts and a water world.

Färjestaden. Tel: (46) 485 392 22. Open: mid-May–Sept daily 10am–6pm. Admission charge.

Ölands Museum

An open-air museum depicting life on the island in the 18th and 19th centuries, including a set of farmhouses with original furniture and farming equipment. There's also an art exhibition of local artists and regional handicrafts, both on display and for sale. Not far from here is a row of the best-preserved windmills for which the island is justly famous.

Himmelsberga. Tel: (46) 485 56 10 22. www.olandsmuseum.com. Open: mid-May–mid-Aug daily 10am–5.30pm; mid-Aug–mid-Sept daily 11am–5pm. Admission charge.

SKÅNE
Bosjökloster Slott

This whitewashed convent was in operation from the 11th century until the Reformation, and today a small museum is housed in the vaulted former refectory, detailing aspects of the building's history. In the early 20th century the building became an aristocratic family home, and the Bonde family, who have lovingly preserved its heritage and condition, still privately run it. The gardens are also of note, featuring a rose garden, a herbarium, grazing animals and a 1,000-year-old oak tree.

Höör. Tel: (46) 413 250 48. www.bosjokloster.se. Castle open: May–Sept daily 10am–6pm. Gardens open: May–Sept daily 8am–8pm; Oct–Apr daily 10am–5pm. Admission charge.

Falsterbo

The most famous building in Falsterbo is its lighthouse, the oldest surviving one in Sweden, dating from 1793. The town is also known in equestrian circles for its annual horse show that takes place every July, and for its migratory birdlife, including raptors and wildfowl, that passes over here every autumn. In July, the town also plays host to classic car races and displays.

Foteviken Viking Centre

Just south of Malmö this Viking Centre re-creates life as it would have been during the great warrior period. The area was very important to the Vikings, and various ancient monuments and archaeological finds that indicate a possible fortress and harbour have been found here. Within this Viking reserve an entire Viking town has been reconstructed including a festivity hall, boats, homes and a smokehouse. Re-enactments of Viking life are also staged here.

Hallörsvägen, Höllviken.
Tel: (46) 40 330 800. www.foteviken.se.

Helsingborg castle tower

Viking Reserve: Open: Jun–Aug daily 10am–4pm; Apr–May & Sept–mid-Oct Mon–Fri 10am–4pm.
Viking Centre: Open: daily 8.30am–4.30pm. Admission charge.

Glimmingehus

Built for a Danish aristocrat in 1499, today Glimmingehus is one of Sweden's best preserved stone medieval homes. Among the treasures that were discovered here by archaeologists in the 20th century were valuable items imported from all over Europe, such as Venetian glass, indicating both the wealth and the extravagance of families that lived here over the centuries. Quirks in its design, such as mysterious holes in walls and traps to ensnare trespassers, add to its appeal, as well as its reputation for being haunted.

Hammenhög. Tel: (46) 414 186 20.
www.raa.se. Open: mid-Apr–May & Sept daily 11am–4pm; Jun–Aug daily 10am–6pm; Oct Sat & Sun noon–4pm.
Admission charge.

Helsingborg

Helsingborg's nickname is 'the pearl of the Sound' because of its waterfront position, and it is indeed a gem of a city, with a lively cultural life and plenty to entertain visitors. Because of its location it was a vital trading city during the Danish occupation in the Middle Ages, but it was also to suffer greatly as a go-between area between the warring Swedish and Danish factions over the centuries. However, by

Götaland

the 19th century, largely helped by the Industrial Revolution, the city began to come into its own. The only real reminder of its medieval heritage is the former castle keep (*kärnan*), which can be climbed for wonderful views of the Öresund Sound.

Dunkers Kulturhus
(Henry Dunker Culture Centre)

One of the most striking buildings on the waterfront is the modern cultural centre designed in 2002 by the architect Kim Utzon. Inside, vast exhibition areas are home to the Helsingborg Museum, detailing the history of the city, an art gallery and a music school. It has already become one of Helsingborg's most popular sights.

Kungsgatan 11. Tel: (46) 421 074 00.
www.dunkerskulturhus.se.
Open: Tue–Sun 10am–5pm (until 8pm
Thur). Admission charge.

Fredriksdal Museum and Gardens

It seems that even the smallest towns in Sweden feel the need to have an open-

The striking Henry Dunker Culture Centre

air museum to preserve their heritage, but Helsingborg's version is among the finest in the country. Centred around an 18th-century manor house are parklands, botanical gardens, animal pastures and a range of preserved buildings.

Gisela Trappsvägatan 1.
Tel: (46) 421 045 00. www.fredriksdal.se.
Open: May & Sept daily 10am–5pm;
Jun–Aug daily 10am–7pm; Oct–Apr
daily 11am–4pm.
Admission charge (free in Jan and Mar).

Sofiero Palace

This former royal summer residence was built in 1864 but was consistently renovated throughout the 19th and 20th centuries. On the instructions of King Gustav VI Adolf, the palace was donated to the town on his death in 1973 and it is now possible to visit the interior rooms and take in the various ornate styles of decoration. The gardens are also impressive and include an orangery and a collection of rhododendrons, a legacy of Gustav Adolf's enthusiasm for the flower.

Sofierovägen.
Tel: (46) 042 14 04 40.
www.sofiero.helsingborg.se.
Park open: Mon–Sat 10am–4pm.
Admission charge.
Palace open: May–Aug daily 11am–5pm.

Lund

Founded in the Middle Ages and, at one time, capital of Denmark, Lund is best known today for its university,

Inside the Kulturen at Lund

established in the mid-17th century. In fact the town even boasts a students' museum dedicated to the history of learning in the city. The most dominant building in the city is the 12th-century cathedral, with its imposing bell towers, but not far from here archaeological finds have proved that a church existed near the site as far back as the 10th century.

Hökieret (Night Hawker's House)

A hawker's house was an establishment set up to serve people too poor to buy goods from larger grocers and shops, but who would come here for a cheap heartening meal such as meatballs or mashed potato, or to buy small helpings of sweets, bread and other comestibles. The building is now a museum, but there is still a shop where visitors can buy old-fashioned sweets and household equipment.
Tel: (46) 463 504 04.
Open: May–Aug daily noon–5pm;
Dec noon–4pm.

Kulturen

Lund's open-air museum has various points of focus, all of which aim to preserve the Swedish rural way of life in the past centuries. Among the attractions are a reconstructed blacksmith's workshop, a 16th-century storehouse, an upper-class Burgher's House, and an 18th-century vicarage. In summer there are also music performances, and a restaurant serves traditional period cuisine, such as sprats and smoked ham.
Tegnersplatsen. Tel: (46) 463 504 00.
www.kulturen.com.
Open: daily 11am–5pm.
Admission charge.

Walk: Malmö

Known as the 'City of Parks' because of its lush greenery divided by a tranquil canal, Malmö is one of the most attractive cities in the country, with its cobbled streets and historic buildings. It makes for a pleasant stroll and most of its sights are within easy walking distance of one another.

Allow about 1 hour for the walk, which covers about 1 km (²/₃ mile). Start at the main square, the Stortorget.

1 Stortorget

Malmö's main square is dominated by a statue of King Karl X Gustav. The Rådhuset (City Hall) and Kockska Huset were both built in the 16th century.
Leave the square at its northeastern corner and continue to Rundelsgatan.

2 St Petri Kyrka (St Peter's Church)

The church still contains a font and pulpit from Renaissance times.
Follow Rundelsgatan to Djäknegatan and turn right, then right again to Lilla Torg.

3 Lilla Torg

This small square has been a meeting place for locals for centuries.

Follow Engelbrektsgatan down to the river, cross the bridge and follow Davidshallsgatan and Radmansgatan and turn right on to St Johannesgata.

4 Malmö Konsthall

One of the largest modern art galleries in Europe, the Malmö art museum building is flooded with natural light.
Turn right on to Pildammsvägen and continue north back over the river on Slottsgatan. Turn left on to the Slotts bron and on to Malmöhusvägen.

5 Malmöhus

Sweden's oldest Renaissance building contains a regional museum, art museum, aquarium and tropicarium.

St Petri Kyrka *Göran Olsgatan 1. Tel: (46) 40 35 90 43.*
Malmö Konsthall *St Johannesgatan 7. Tel: (46) 40 34 12 93. www.konsthall.malmo.se. Open: daily 11am–5pm (to 9pm Wed). Free admission.*
Malmöhus *Malmöhusvägen 1. Tel: (46) 40 34 44 37. www.malmo.se/museer. Open: Jun–Aug daily 10am–4pm; Sept–May daily noon–4pm. Admission charge.*

Kommendanthuset *Malmöhusvägen 1. Tel: (46) 40 34 44 39. www.malmo.se/museer. Open: Jun–Aug daily 10am–4pm, Sept–May daily noon–4pm. Admission charge.*
Teknikens och Sjöfartens Hus *Malmöhusvägen 1. Tel: (46) 40 34 44 38. www.malmo.se/museer. Open: Jun–Aug daily 10am–4pm; Sept–May daily noon–4pm. Admission charge.*

Cross Malmöhusvägen to the opposite side of the road.

6 Kommendanthuset

The former residence of the castle's commandant is now a museum.
Continue west along Malmöhusvägen.

7 Teknikens och Sjöfartens Hus (Science and Maritime Centre)

A haven for science fanatics, including a flight simulator and submarine.
Follow Tessins Väg to Regementsgatan, then turn right up Sergels Väg.

8 Ribersborg Beach

This lovely sandy beach offers safe swimming waters and a string of outdoor cafés.
Follow Limhamnsvägen to the junction with Mariedallsvägen, then cross the bridge and walk up Västra Varvsgatan. Turn left on to Lilla Varvsgatan then Scania platsen.

9 Turning Torso

Sweden's tallest building, designed by Santiago Calatrava, twists 90 degrees from top to bottom.

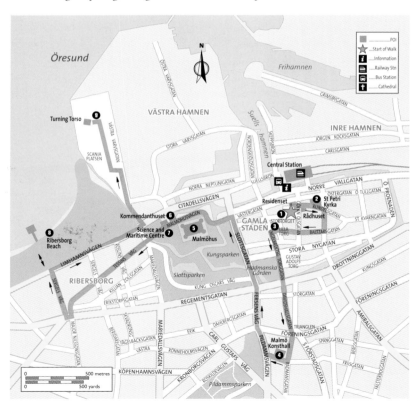

Designed by Santiago Calatrava, the Turning Torso in Malmö twists 90 degrees

ÖRESUND BRIDGE

The idea of a bridge linking Sweden and Denmark had been a moot point for around 100 years, but the Öresund Bridge was finally constructed and opened in June 2000. The 8km (5-mile) cable-stayed bridge is the longest of its kind in the world and links Malmö with Denmark. The 204m (669ft) pylons supporting the cables are visible from far and wide. The bridge has two layers – the upper one for motor traffic and the lower one for the railway line that runs between Malmö and Copenhagen. Every year the Bridge Run attracts marathon runners from around the world to sprint across the bridge from the artificial island of Peberholm in Denmark to Malmö Stadium.

Östarp

Two farmsteads, one dating from 1812 and the other from 1907, have been protected complete with furniture, textiles and tools in this open-air museum to keep traditional peasant culture alive. Native livestock, ancient farming techniques and other features of rural life are explained here, while during the summer visitors can participate in activities such as haymaking and threshing.
Tel: (46) 468 0407. Open: May–Aug Tue–Sun 11am–5pm; Sept Sat & Sun 11am–5pm. Admission charge.

Ven

During spring and summer the small island of Ven, nestling in the waters between Sweden and Denmark, is a popular holiday resort, with good beaches and bicycle trails and various artists' studios. In the 16th century the island was home to the celebrated Danish astronomer Tycho Brahe who established a castle and an observatory here. High up on a hill is the 12th-century church of St Ibb, which includes an original baptismal font.

Ystad

Unusually for a country whose wooden buildings have so often been destroyed by fire, Ystad has managed to preserve more than 300 half-timbered buildings that give the town a unique atmosphere, all the more evocative at night when the streets are floodlit by old-fashioned lamps. One of the loveliest buildings is the Franciscan monastery dating from 1267.

Ales Stenar

Just outside Ystad is one of the country's most impressive Viking sites, a stone ship outline of 60 monoliths. Although archaeologists are not yet clear what the symbolism of the site can be, the general opinion is that the 67m (220ft) long outline was constructed to commemorate a ship's crew lost at sea.

SMÅLAND
Astrid Lindgrens Värld (Astrid Lindgren's World)

The best-known creation of children's writer Astrid Lindgren, who was born near Vimmerby, is Pippi Longstocking, an eccentric little girl with pigtails who lives on her own in a yellow cottage. Other characters include a farm boy called Emil, the castle-dwelling Ronja, the Robber's Daughter and the Children of Noisy Village. In this theme park for children, all the characters and their homes and adventures are brought to life. There is also an Astrid Lindgren Centre that details her life and work. *Vimmerby. Tel: (46) 492 798 00. www.alv.se. Open: mid-May–mid-Jun daily 10am–5pm; mid-Jun–Aug daily 10am–6pm; Sept–mid-Oct Sat & Sun 10am–5pm. Admission charge.*

Blå Jungfrun

This island, off the coast of Oskarshamn, is shrouded in mystery. Legend has it that all witches fly here at Easter time on their broomsticks to visit Blåkulla, home of the witches. The island is now a national park containing caves and a stone labyrinth, and boats make regular ferry trips here during the summer.

Eksjö

The whole town of Eksjö has become a listed site because of its wonderful wooden architecture, much of which dates from the 17th century. The town is also strongly associated with the army, as it has been used as a military training area since the 15th century.

The Eksjö Museums

The full history of the town is explored here by bringing to life characters from different centuries, such as a 17th-century ox dealer and an 18th-century mayor. As their 'lives' unfold, a sense of what it is like to live in Eksjö in

ASTRID LINDGREN

Astrid Lindgren was born in the farming village of Näs in 1907 and grew up to become one of the few Swedish writers to achieve a truly international reputation, with her work translated into 86 languages. At the age of 38 she began writing the children's stories that would capture the imagination of every Swedish child and other kids around the world, set in the region in which Astrid grew up, although she spent her adult years in Stockholm. The first Pippi Longstocking tale was published in 1945 and became an instant success, leading to a lifelong career writing over 100 books. After her death in 2002, the Swedish government set up the Astrid Lindgren Memorial Award in her honour, which is now the highest-paid award for children's literature in the world.

different periods starts to emerge. There's also a permanent exhibit devoted to the locally born artist Albert Engström (1869–1940).
*Österlänggatan 31.
Tel: (46) 381 361 60.
Open: July–Aug Mon–Fri 11am–6pm, Sat & Sun 11am–3pm; Sept–Jun Tue–Fri 1–5pm, Sat & Sun 11am–3pm.
Admission charge.*

Gränna

Gränna was created by Count Per Brahe in 1632, and it soon became a thriving town, particularly because of its temperate climate, which allowed locals to become self-sufficient in vegetables and fruit (especially the Gränna pear). Just north of the town are the ruins of the count's castle, Brahehus, which was destroyed by fire in 1708. One of the most popular souvenirs, seen all over town, is the red-and-white mint-flavoured candy rock known as *polkagris*.

Gränna Museum–Andrée Expedition Polarcenter

This museum is dedicated to the ill-fated polar expedition undertaken by Solomon Andrée in 1897. Andrée, in the company of two others, set off on a research trip to the North Pole from Gränna in a hot-air balloon called *The Eagle*. The balloon crashed fatally on White Island, a fact which was discovered only 30 years later. As well as a detailed reconstruction of this expedition, made possible by the discovery of Andrée's diaries and photographs, the museum also documents all subsequent research trips to the Arctic and their importance in helping us understand this inhospitable area.

Götaland

Ruins of the castle Brahehus in Gränna

Brahegatan 38–40. Tel: (46) 36 10 38 90.
www.grennamuseum.se.
Open: mid-May–Aug daily 10am–6pm;
Sept–mid-May daily 10am–4pm.
Admission charge.

Jönköping

An important trading town since the
Middle Ages, this is now a lively
university town with plenty of
restaurants and cafés to suit all
tastes. In the 19th century
Jönköping became best known
for its production of safety matches.
It is still often referred to as the
'matchstick town'.

Jönköpings Läns Museum
(Jönköping County Museum)

The renowned Swedish artist John Bauer
was born in Jönköping, so fittingly the
region's main museum has the largest
collection of his works. Bauer is best
known for his romantic images of
Swedish folklore, depicting trolls and
princesses in a fairy-tale landscape of
forests and grottoes. Other permanent
exhibits detail the town's 700-year history.
Dag Hammarskjölds plats 2.
Tel: (46) 36 30 18 00. www.jkpglm.se.
Open: Tue–Sun 11am–5pm (until 8pm
Wed; also July–Aug Mon 11am–5pm).
Admission charge.

The fairy-tale castle of Kalmar Slott

Tändstickmuseet (Match Museum)

The only museum in the world dedicated to the production of matches is housed in a former matchstick factory. Equipment and the history of the industry, including the lives of those who worked here and their living quarters, are all explored, while the museum shop has a wonderful array of old matchboxes and posters bringing back the glory days of illustrated labels. *Tändstickgränd 27. Tel: (46) 36 10 55 43. Open: Jun–Aug Mon–Fri 10am–5pm, Sat & Sun 10am–3pm; Sept–May Tue–Sat 11am–3pm. Admission charge (free Nov–Feb).*

Kalmar

One of Sweden's oldest cities is worth a day's stroll around its cobbled streets, soaking up the historical atmosphere. In the evening the town comes alive with its many bars and restaurants, particularly around the main square.

Kalmar Läns Museum (Kalmar County Museum)

The full and complex history of Kalmar is documented in the town's county museum – from its Bronze Age archaeological finds and its medieval importance, to local artists from the 19th century. One of the highlights is the salvaged gold treasure from the wreck of the royal ship *Kronan* which sank at the end of the 17th century and was only discovered in 1980. Much of the activities at the museum are geared towards children, including the chance to dress up in 19th-century costumes and participate in tasks such as baking bread and churning butter as they would have been done 100 years ago. *Skeppsbrogatan 51. Tel: (46) 480 45 13 00. www.kalmarlansmuseum.se. Open: Jun–Aug daily 10am–6pm; Sept–May Mon–Fri 10am–4pm, Sat & Sun 11am–4pm. Admission charge.*

Kalmar Slott

Kalmar's castle dates back 800 years, when it was built as a defence against seafaring invaders, particularly from Denmark. In the 16th century it was entirely renovated in the Renaissance style. The most important event at the castle, in a historical context, was the signing of the Kalmar Union in 1397, which united Denmark, Norway and Sweden under one sovereignty (*see p13*). *Kungsgatan 1. Tel: (46) 480 451 490. www.kalmarslott.kalmar.se. Open: May–Jun & Sept daily 10am–4pm; July–Aug 10am–5pm; Oct–Apr times vary. Admission charge.*

Karlshamn

Originally a small village called Bodekull, this harbour town was renamed after King Karl X Gustav when he gave it a town charter in 1668 because of its suitability for transporting wood. One of the most distinctive features of the town today is the 18th-century houses fronted by painted pillars. From the town's pretty harbour there are various boat trips, including those to the island of Frisholmen to visit the 17th-century citadel that was built to defend the town. The area also draws avid anglers to the salmon-rich River Mörrum between April and July.

Karlshamn Museum

Karlshamn developed a worldwide reputation for the Flagg Punsch that it produced during the 18th and 19th centuries. This former punch factory is now dedicated to showcasing the production and export of this popular alcoholic drink. The owner of the factory also produced playing cards, snuff and tobacco, and old manufacturing equipment can still be seen here. Also within the museum are various preserved merchants' homes, a printing works and an old silversmith's.
Vinkelgatan 8. Tel: (46) 454 148 68.
www.karlshamnsmuseum.se.
Open: May–Sept Mon–Fri 1pm–5pm;
Oct–Apr Mon–Fri 1–4pm.
Admission charge.

Karlskrona

Designated a UNESCO World Heritage Site since 1998, Karlskrona became an important naval base in the late 17th century. The original dockyards (Gamla Örlogssvarvet), flanked by Sweden's largest wooden church, are now preserved, while inland the town is a beautiful example of the Baroque architecture so popular during the 18th century. This is especially apparent in the main square (Stortorget), where

two Baroque churches, with their bell towers and dome respectively, grace the landscape.

Blekinge Museum

Set in a row of protected houses, the Karlskrona county museum examines life in the region through the ages. As well as exploring the local fishing and mining industries, life in general for both rich and poor during the glory days of the 18th century is another area of emphasis.
Borgmästaregatan 21. Tel: (46) 455 30
49 85. Open: mid-Jun–mid-Aug daily
10am–6pm; mid-Aug–mid-Jun Tue–Sun
11am–5pm (until 7pm Wed). Admission
charge.

Marinmuseum (Maritime Museum)

The importance of the naval industry to Karlskrona was recognised as far back as 1752 when the king requested that a small museum be established here to preserve the history of the shipping trade. Ship building and maritime trade remain the primary focus of the exhibits, but there are also fascinating sections devoted to warships, including a reconstruction of an 18th-century gun deck, and an underwater transparent tunnel where a wreck and its resultant marine life can be seen.
Stumholmen. Tel: (46) 455 35 93 02.
www.marinmuseum.se.
Open: Jan–mid-Jun Tue–Sun
11am–5pm; mid-Jun–mid-Aug daily
10am–6pm. Admission charge.

The Marinmuseum, by royal request

Drive: Kingdom of crystal

Between Växjö and Nybro is an area commonly referred to as the 'kingdom of crystal' because of the many glassworks factories located in the region. Whether you are simply interested in purchasing a piece to take home as a souvenir or are curious to discover how the products are made, this makes for a pleasant day's drive.

The route covers around 60km (37 miles), but allow a full day to stop off at the workshops.

Most of the factory shops offer substantial discounts. From June to August visitors can have a go at blowing and painting glass. (*Guided tours & demonstrations at the workshops: July daily; May–Jun & Aug–Sept Mon–Sat; admission charge.*) *Start on road No 25 at Hovmantorp and take the first left turning to reach Bergdala.*

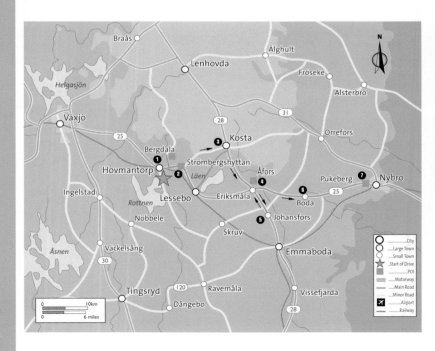

1 Bergdala

Bergdala is best known for its blue-edged glass, spiral stems and depictions of Vikings and elks. The factory has barely changed its appearance since it opened in the late 19th century.

Return to road No 25 and continue east to Strömbergshyttan.

2 Studioglas Strömbergshyttan

This innovative glass studio opened in 1987 and quickly became one of the most inspired, with new techniques and quirky yet desirable items.

Continue southeast to Lessebo and take the left turning to the road No 28, following it northward to Kosta.

3 Kosta

The oldest glass factory in the country includes a museum about the industry.

Drive southward to Åfors.

4 Åfors

The most innovative designs are created here, with well-known designers such as Gunnel Sahlin.

Continue south on road No 28 to Johansfors.

5 Johansfors

Elegant crystal pieces are the trademark of this glassworks factory, but there are also more contemporary items decorated with abstract designs.

Backtrack to the junction of road Nos 28 and 25 and follow No 25 east until you see a left-hand turning directing you to Boda.

Bergdala
Tel: (46) 478 316 50. Open: Mon–Fri 10am–5pm, Sat & Sun 10am–4pm.
Studioglas Strömbergshyttan
Tel: (46) 478 310 75. Open: Mon–Fri 9am–4pm, Sat 10am–4pm, Sun noon–4pm.
Kosta
Tel: (46) 478 345 00. Open: Mon–Fri 9am–6pm, Sat 10am–4pm, Sun noon–4pm.
Åfors
Tel: (46) 481 342 74. Open: Mon–Fri 9am–6pm, Sat 10am–5pm, Sun 11am–5pm.
Johanfors
Kvarnvägen 2. Tel: (46) 471 402 70. Open: Mon–Fri 10am–5pm, Sat 10am–4pm, Sun noon–4pm.
Boda
Tel: (46) 481 424 10. Open: Mon–Fri 9am–6pm, Sat 10am–4pm, Sun noon–4pm.
Pukeberg
Nybro. Tel: (46) 481 800 29. Open: Mon–Fri 9am–5pm, Sat 10am–3pm (also May–Aug Sun noon–4pm).

6 Boda

Bright colours and intricate patterns are the distinctions of the Boda pieces.

Return to road No 25 and continue east to Pukeberg.

7 Pukeberg

Pukeberg is generally known for its classic designs in sandblasted glass.

Crystal pieces

Swedish design

Sweden, like the rest of Scandinavia, has a long tradition of handicrafts practised by local people over the centuries. It was at the end of the 19th century, however, that these talents emerged into the world of functional yet elegant household furniture and other design items.

At the end of the 19th century Carl Larsson (*see p23*) captured the hearts of fellow Swedes with the publication of *Ett Hem* (At Home), which featured his illustrations of home life filled with pale wood furniture, cheerful textiles and a sense of airiness. It gave rise to a movement referred to as 'beauty for all', meaning that elegant and well-thought-out interiors should be accessible to everyone and not just the wealthy. From this also arose the concept that art could be wedded with industry – that is, mass-produced items need not lose quality for quantity. Items needed to be multifunctional as well; a bench by day, for example, would convert into a bed by night.

After home-grown success, Swedish design began to inspire an international audience in the 1920s and 1930s, when a series of World Fairs introduced the masterful designs of the country's glassblowers. Swedish glass design is still considered among the world's finest. One of the major factors of Swedish design is its use of natural materials, so wood, glass (from sand), wool and silver play a major role. Pine and birch, for example, are not only abundant in the Swedish forests but also provide high-quality sturdy wood, ideal for furniture and other carpentry items.

Many Swedish designers have made their name in furniture design, but from the 1940s until his death in 1988, Bruno Mathsson was one of Sweden's most successful and influential. His trademark was bent-wood chairs, such as 'The Grasshopper' which went on to become an international classic. Of course, in recent years, the Swedish

Glass pieces by Kerstin Paulsrud

Ikea flags flying high outside the store

influence in our homes has taken over the world with the emergence of Ikea, offering attractive designs at bargain prices.

In ceramics and pottery too, Sweden has made its mark. The country's most famous porcelain factory is Rörstrand in Linköping, established in the 18th century. Their Swedish Grace range of crockery, inspired by the simplicity of the landscape, is as popular today as it was at its inception in 1930.

In the post-war period two other factors came into play in the development of design. Life had gained in pace and women were no longer strictly housebound, so items needed to be even more functional to speed up previously laborious chores. In addition, the world was increasingly turning to electronics and plastics, so companies such as Ericsson and Electrolux emerged with equipment that was both innovative and practical.

Fashion, too, has reached the masses from its Swedish roots, with companies like H&M (Hennes and Mauritz) now boasting more than 1,000 stores worldwide.

SWEDISH INVENTIONS

Sweden has not only been innovative in aesthetics, but has branched out into the fields of industry, science and medicine. Swedish scientists, inventors and entrepreneurs are responsible for giving the world the following items that now form a part of our everyday life: the Celsius thermometer; telephone handsets and digital telephones; the monkey wrench; the safety match; dynamite; frozen vegetables; the intravenous drip; the pacemaker; kidney dialysis machines; asthma inhalers; the three-point seat belt; the blow torch; synthetic diamonds; the Hasselblad camera; and children's car seats.

Västervik

Beautiful flower-decked wooden houses
and blue waters are what make
Västervik stand out, and the town is
extremely popular as a summer resort,
offering swimming and boating, as well
as fishing activities. The town's central
museum details its history from the
Stone Age, through the emergence of
the shipbuilding industry in the 16th
century, to the present day.

Västervik Museum: Kulbacken.
Tel: (46) 490 211 77.
www.vasterviksmuseum.se.
Open: Tue–Fri 11am–4pm, Sun 1–4pm.
Admission charge.

Växjö

Culture and art are the main concerns
of modern-day Växjö, with a renowned
chamber orchestra and theatre, as well
as a lively student population attending
the town's renowned university.

The picture-perfect town of Västervik

FAMINE AND EMIGRATION

Between 1866 and 1868, known as the
'starvation years', many Swedes, particularly
those in the largely agricultural area of
Småland, were subjected to extreme weather
conditions that ruined their crops and
resulted in first famine and then disease. With
the tandem growth of shipping traffic across
the Atlantic, many travelled to Gothenburg
where they boarded liners bound for the
United States. The journey took around three
weeks to the port of New York, where many
continued onward, to the states of Illinois and
Minnesota. In addition to a new language and
a new culture, many of the immigrants faced
further challenges in adapting from a rural
life to an urban one, with the largest Swedish
community establishing itself in Chicago.
Hardships were overcome, however, and by
the turn of the 20th century one fifth of all
Swedes lived in the United States.

Utvandrarnas Hus
(House of Emigrants)

Between 1850 and 1930 more than one
million Swedes emigrated to the United
States in search of a better life. The
'Dream of America' exhibition here
documents all aspects of their
experiences, from the arduous journey
to the cultural and physical hardships
and challenges they faced on arrival.
Another exhibition examines the work
of the Nobel-Prize-winning author
Vilhelm Moberg, whose trilogy *The
Emigrants* (1949–59) was one of the
most evocative works on the struggle of
Swedish immigrants in America. There
is also an institute that includes
archives of immigrants' personal
experiences and photographs, and a
research centre where resident or

returning Swedes can trace their family tree.

Vilhelm Mobergs gata 4.
Tel: (46) 470 201 20.
www.utvandrarnashus.se.
Open: May–Aug Mon–Fri 9am–5pm,
Sat & Sun 11am–4pm; Sept–Apr
Tue–Fri 9am–4pm, Sat 11am–4pm.
Admission charge.

Smålands Museum

Glassblowing has long been associated with Småland. Within the provincial museum the traditions and development of the craft are uncovered in full and remain the most popular part of the museum. Other exhibits include a collection of coins, textiles, historic furniture and church ornaments.
Södra Järnvägsgatan 2.

Tel: (46) 470 70 42 00.
www.smalandsmuseum.se.
Open: Jun–Aug Mon–Fri 10am–5pm,
Sat & Sun 11am–5pm; Sept–May
Tue–Fri 10am–5pm, Sat & Sun
11am–5pm. Admission charge.

WESTERN GÖTALAND
Borås

Set up in the 17th century as a trading centre for the local textile industry, Borås today keeps this tradition of peddling alive through the large number of mail-order companies based here. Borås is also known for its many parks which burst into bloom during the summer months, scenting the air.

Borås Djurpark (Borås Zoo)

Right in the centre of town is this large zoo that boasts natural habitats for a

Cycling is popular among locals in Götaland

Dalsand Canal

large number of species. The heart of the zoo is the African savannah where monkeys, rhinos and other animals from the continent roam. The zoo also operates various successful breeding programmes and is home to the only elephants to have been born on Swedish soil.
Tel: (46) 33 35 32 70.
www.borasdjurpark.se.
Open: daily 10am–4pm (until 6pm Jun–Aug). Admission charge.

Textilmuseet
(Textile History Museum)
The centuries of textile trading in Borås are uncovered in this specially dedicated museum. Among the exhibits are old spinning wheels, examples of cloth and clothing, and historical photographs.
Druveforsvägen 8. Tel: (46) 33 35 89 50.

Open: Tue & Thur 10am–8pm, Wed & Fri 10am–4pm, Sat & Sun noon–4pm. Admission charge.

Dalsand Canal
One of the most dominant sights along this verdant waterway is the Håverud Aqueduct, a steel edifice constructed to cross the 9m (30ft) waterfall and gorge. Also of note are the rock carvings at Högsbyn dating back 3,000 years and depicting ancient boats and Stone Age figures. Ferries ply the canal daily past undulating countryside and small towns while navigating the 19 locks, which makes for a peaceful day trip.

Falkenberg
Set on the banks of the River Ätran, much of Falkenberg's Old Town area has been preserved, but it is also a lively

modern town of fashionable bars, cafés and shops. One of the charms of the town's main museum is that it recreates historical furnishings from a more recent past than most of Sweden's folk museums – there is a fully furnished 1950s apartment here. Surrounding the town are beaches, farmland, forests and waterways, earning it the title 'Sweden in miniature'.

Fjällbacka

Flanked by the 70m (230ft) mountain Vetteberget, it is Fjällbacka's harbourfront that is the focus of the town's activities, particularly during the herring-fishing season. This popular tourist resort was a favourite with the Swedish actress turned Hollywood star Ingrid Bergman (*see p25*) and a statue of her now stands in the square named in her honour.

Gunnebo Slott (Gunnebo House)

Often referred to as the most beautiful wooden building in the world, Gunnebo House was built in the neoclassical style in the 18th century for a wealthy local merchant. It was designed by the architect Carl Wilhelm Carlberg, who designed much of nearby Gothenburg, with remarkable attention to detail, including ceramic stoves, parquet flooring and external stone friezes. Thanks to detailed architectural drawings for the original house, an intensive restoration project was undertaken in the 1990s, including the construction of servants' quarters that were part of the original design but never completed. Carlberg also

The beautiful gardens and lake by Gunnebo Slott

designed the gardens in the English style popular at the time and a farm that allowed the estate to be self-sufficient.
Tel: (46) 31 334 16 00.
www.gunneboslott.se.
Open: May–mid-Jun & Sept Sat & Sun noon–2pm; mid-Jun–Aug daily noon–2pm; Oct–Apr Sun noon–1pm.
Admission charge.

Halmstad

One of the landmarks in this west-coast town is the large *Woman's Head* sculpture by Picasso beside the river. The town's wooden architecture has also been preserved. Another popular sight, which dates back to the 13th century, is the moored training ship *Najaden*. On Lilla Torg a former workhouse has now been converted into the Fattighuset, a centre for local handicrafts.

Halmstad Äventyrsland (Halmstad Adventure Land)

Entirely geared towards children, this theme park covers a diverse number of subjects, from the dinosaur park with life-size models, a pirate land, a saga park re-creating many of Sweden's myths and fairy tales, and Miniland, where models of the country's most famous buildings have been reproduced in miniature.
Gamla Tylösandsvägen 1.
Tel: (46) 35 10 84 60.
Open: May–Sept daily 10am–8pm.
Admission charge.

A pretty wooden house in Hjo

Hjo

The lakeside town of Hjo is known throughout the country for the charming sight of pretty wooden houses painted in bright colours and fronted by ornate verandahs and cherry trees. The town has also been a popular spa resort since the end of the 19th century. One of the most relaxing summer activities is to take a steamboat tour on the lake aboard the 1892 SS *Trafik*, which also offers evening jazz cruises.

Karlsborg

The town of Karlsborg was originally constructed with its city walls as a defence measure in the centre of the country but was never required to fulfil its original purpose. Today the town stands within its walls largely as a tourist attraction, and stunt shows with special effects in summer re-create 19th-century life.

Koster Islands

Joined together under the banner of a nature reserve, this archipelago is noted for fine beaches, inland moors and opportunities for swimming, cycling and hiking. Lovers of shellfish will also enjoy the many cosy waterfront restaurants serving up lobsters and oysters fresh from the sea.

Kungälv

The beautiful coastline, moors and the charming cobbled streets of Kungälv's old town area all contribute to its popularity as a summer resort. The town is dominated by the 700-year-old Bohus Fortress. It was restored during the 20th century and today visitors can see the former prison cells and cannons. During the summer re-enactments of historical events are staged in the grounds.

Läckö Slott (Läckö Castle)

The largest castle in Sweden, and its most beautiful, Läckö Slott was built in the 13th century but much of its decoration today owes itself to a refurbishment in the 16th century and a restoration in the 20th. Some 200 rooms are presented with their plush Baroque furnishings, while the kitchen is a wonderful step back in time to the foods and cooking traditions of days gone by. One of the highlights of the year is the summer opera season held in front of the castle.
Tel: (46) 510 48 46 60.
www.lackoslott.se.
Open: May daily 11am–5pm; Jun–Aug

Götaland

Läckö Slott is considered to be one of the most stunning castles in Sweden

*daily 11am–6pm; Sept Mon–Fri
11am–3pm. Admission charge.*

Husaby

Considered the birthplace of
Christianity in Sweden, it was here that
the first Christian king Olof Skötkonung
was baptised by a British monk in about
the year 1000. In the 12th century a
church was erected at the site of the
baptism, becoming the country's first
cathedral. The vaulted interior is
beautifully decorated with ceiling
frescoes and chandeliers. The well where
the baptism is said to have taken place
can still be seen just north of the church.

Lidköping

Most people are drawn to Lidköping for
its discount factory outlets selling
bargain-priced porcelain that has long
been produced in the town. But it is also
a pleasant place to stroll around, with
plenty of cafés and shops and a laid-
back atmosphere. Much of the original
town was lost during a fire in the 19th
century but some old timber buildings
still survive around Limtorget.

Vänermuseet (Väner Museum)

All aspects of life on Lake Vänern are
explored here, including fossilised
finds, local fish species and a history of
the shipping industry that has been a
mainstay for centuries.
*Framnäsvågen 2. Tel: (46) 510 77 00 65.
Open: Tue–Fri 10am–5pm, Sat & Sun
noon–5pm (also Jun–Aug Mon
10am–5pm). Admission charge.*

Lysekil

Set within a stunning landscape of
fjords, Lysekil has been a popular
summer resort since the 19th century,
with its wide beach and wonderful
views. As well as safe swimming,
the area is ideal for cycling
and fishing.

Havets Hus

For an area that has relied so much on
fishing for its livelihood, it's not
surprising to find an aquarium that
gives visitors an idea of the wealth of
the region's coastal waters. Here, local
species such as cod, halibut and lobster
can be seen in a vast cylindrical tank.
What's more, the water for the tank is
pumped directly from the Gullmafjord,
so the fish are surviving almost entirely
in their natural habitat.
*Tel: (46) 523 668 161.
www.havetshus.lysekil.se. Open: mid-
Jun–mid-Aug daily 10am–6pm; mid-
Aug–Oct & mid-Feb–mid-Jun daily
10am–4pm. Admission charge.*

Nordens Ark

The primary aim of this zoo and nature
park is the preservation of endangered
species through breeding programmes
and research, but it remains a popular
tourist attraction nonetheless.
Both Scandinavian species and those
from around the world are of
importance here, including wolverines,
leopards and pandas.
*Aby Säteri, Hunnebostrand.
Tel: (46) 523 795 90. www.nordensark.se.*

Open: Oct–Mar daily 10am–4pm; Apr–mid-Jun & mid-Aug–Sept daily 10am–5pm; mid-Jun–mid-Aug daily 10am–7pm. Last entry is one hour before closing time. Admission charge.

Skara

The most prominent feature of Skara is the Gothic cathedral built in the 11th century and decorated with beautiful stained-glass windows. The town is also a real draw for families, being home to the largest amusement park in Scandinavia. Most of the activities are water-based, including slides, canoeing and water-skiing, but there is also a zoo and the opportunity to try one's hand at panning for gold.

Smögen

Smögen is best known for its fish auction, the second largest in the country, which is held every day when the fishermen return with their catch of prawns and other shellfish. The harbour is a constant hive of activity and is lined with cafés in wonderfully preserved wooden buildings. At the end of the quay is a fisherman's cottage from the 19th century that is still furnished as it would have been in the 1850s.

Tanum

The Bronze Age rock carvings in Tanum are its most famous feature and have now been designated a UNESCO

Houses along Smögen harbour

World Heritage Site. Over a vast area some 10,000 carved figures have now been linked with footpaths so that visitors can get the full experience. The sheer number of the carvings means that a very clear and full picture of life at the time can be ascertained, including methods of transportation and hunting, and the belief systems involving gods and spirits. The largest rock carving in the group can now be seen in the town's **Vitlycke Museum**.
Museum: Vitlycke 2.
Tel: (46) 525 209 50. Open: Apr–Sept daily 10am–6pm. Admission charge.

Tjolöholms Slott

Probably the most incongruous building in Sweden, this Tudor-style house looks as though it's been plucked straight from the English countryside. It was, in fact, built for a Scottish businessman at the turn of the 20th century. As well as its striking exterior, inside there are many remarkable features. Hot-air pipes heated the house, the bathrooms included showers, and the carpets were vacuumed by inserting hosepipes through the window and having a draught horse pull the suction machinery from outside.
Stiftelsen Tjolöholm, Fjärås.
Tel: (46) 300 40 46 00.
www.tjoloholm.se. Open: Apr–mid-Jun & Sept Sat & Sun 11am–4pm; mid-Jun–Aug daily 11am–4pm; Sept Sat & Sun noon–3pm; Oct Sun noon–3pm. Admission charge.

Tjörn

Linked to the mainland by its famous bridge, Tjörn is a haven for swimming, cycling and trekking. The island is thought to have been inhabited some 2,000 years ago, after Stone Age rock carvings were found here. In more recent times the island has been the focus of a herring fishing industry. Culturally the most popular sight on the island is the **Nordiska Akvarellmuseet** (Nordic Watercolour Museum), which not only displays watercolours by Scandinavian and international artists but also runs courses on the techniques of the medium.
Museum: Södra Hamnen 6, Skärhamn.
Tel: (46) 304 60 00 80.
www.akvarellmuseet.org. Open: Jun–Sept 11am–6pm; Oct–May Tue–Sun noon–5pm (until 8pm Thur). Admission charge.

Uddevalla

With its forested backdrop and attractive harbour Uddevalla has long been a lively and attractive community. The town was once renowned for shipbuilding, and in the Bohusläns Museum much of the focus is on this industry, with displays of old fishing fleets, as well as depictions of the lives of the local fishermen in the area over the centuries. Other exhibitions here reflect local arts and crafts.
Museum: Museigatau 1.
Tel: (46) 522 65 65 00.
www.bohuslansmuseum.se. Open: May–Aug Mon–Thur 10am–8pm,

Fri–Sun 10am–4pm; Sept–Apr closed Mon. Free admission.

Vänersborg

On the south side of Lake Vänern, Vänersborg has been inhabited for more than 7,000 years, as attested by archaeological finds. The town is often referred to as 'Little Paris' after the poems of its native-born son Birger Sjöberg who, despite moving away, continued to write about his home town under this title. With its lakeside location, it is an ideal summer spot for swimming and fishing.

Kungajaktmuseet Älgens Berg (Hunneberg Royal Hunt Museum)

Just outside Vänersborg are the hills of Hunneberg and Halleberg, home to a large group of elk and the scene of an annual royal hunt. This museum details the history of the hunt as well as providing facts and figures about elk and other fauna, and the geology of the region.

Hunneberg. Tel: (46) 521 27 79 91. Open: Jun–Aug daily 11am–6pm; Sept–May Tue–Sun 11am–4pm. Admission charge.

Varberg

This lovely coastal town has been thriving since the Middle Ages, and in the 19th century gained a further reputation as a spa resort. The intricate design of the therapeutic baths is still a major feature of the town. The most prominent landmark of the town is the 13th-century fortress, inside which there is now a museum, the Länmuseet Varbergs Fästning, detailing the history of the town.

An unusual oriental-style sauna in Varberg

The humble herring

Every country has a culinary speciality that marks it out from other nations, and for Sweden it has to be the humble herring, which not only feeds its own people in abundance, but is a large part of the export economy. Baltic herring (*Clupea harengus membras*), found off Sweden's east coast in copious amounts, has been a staple of the Swedish diet for centuries: herring bones have even been discovered by archaeologists during digs of Neolithic sites. The

Soused herring (*matjessill*)

Baltic herring is smaller than its counterpart the Atlantic herring and is drawn to these waters because of the low salinity.

One of the primary reasons for its popularity, aside from its large numbers and therefore easy catch, is that it is possible to preserve the fish in salt or ferment it, which in days gone by made it a year-round delicacy, able to be eaten even in winter when the hunting and fishing seasons were over. In addition, the oily fish is extremely high in nutrients and fatty acids that make it one of the healthiest items on the Swedish menu. It only requires around 80g (3oz) of salted herring per day to ensure the necessary protein to survive the long winter months.

The prime time for fishing for herring is spring and autumn when shoals of the fish congregate in the waters off the Swedish coast. Once the fish is caught, if it is not to be served fresh, it is gutted and then cured in brine and stored in large barrels for months. Once it is ready to use it is soaked in water or milk to remove excess salt, then served either raw, cooked or pickled. Its versatility adds to its appeal, lending itself to grilling, frying, smoking or baking.

Herring being smoked

The most common way that visitors to Sweden will experience herring is in its many guises as part of a *smörgåsbord* (*see p173*), or as another favourite, particularly in winter, as part of a herring and potato casserole (*sillgratin*). Another speciality is the rollmop, in which a cured fillet is rolled up, marinated in vinegar and flavoured with onion, cucumber and mustard.

A delicacy of northern Sweden is *surströmming* (literally 'sour herring'), a dish of fermented herring that is definitely an acquired taste. The method of fermenting fish was invented centuries ago when the cost of salt was too high for the use of the curing technique. The fish are caught in the spring then fermented in tins for about six months, during which time gases build up and the tin begins to bulge. The traditional time to start eating *surströmming*, therefore, is when the first leaves begin to fall from the trees – the delicacy is not sold until the third Thursday in August, which is known as the *surströmming* premiere. Once the tin is opened, an overwhelming odour of gaseous, rotted fish is released, and for this reason it is traditional to eat the meal outdoors. The dish is served rolled up in thin square-shaped bread (*tunnbröd*), with boiled potatoes, chopped onions and sour cream, and washed down with either milk, schnapps, *aquavit* or beer.

Gotland

Gotland is Sweden's largest island, set in the middle of the Baltic Sea, 90km (56 miles) from the mainland. It offers a range of experiences, from long, isolated beaches to inland wildernesses, and natural fruit orchards to rocky cliffs ideal for birdwatching. Historically, Gotland has been important since Viking times, as the many archaeological finds here prove, while its capital, Visby, has been designated a World Heritage Site by UNESCO.

Bro Kyrka (Bro Church)

Dating from the 13th century, Bro's Church is believed to be constructed on the site of a former sacred fountain. Of note are animal reliefs and beautiful sculptures depicting the Nativity and the Annunciation, as well as original frescoes above the chancel showing Christ, St John the Baptist, St Bartholomew and St Olav. At the base of the choir are 18th-century wood paintings depicting Adam and Eve in the Garden of Eden.

Open: May–Sept daily 8am–6pm. Free admission.

Bunge

The most prominent feature of Bunge is the 14th-century Gothic church. Inside are limestone paintings in Germanic style depicting battles between knights and pirates. Also of

Enjoy the clear blue skies, mild climate and fresh air in Gotland

note is the alms box, also in limestone, decorated with rune inscriptions.

Bungemuseet

Sweden is rife with open-air museums, but this is one of the largest. By accumulating buildings from different parts of the island, such as mills, stables and workshops, life in Gotland over the past 300 years can be explored in a 'living' atmosphere. Also in the museum are rune stones dating from the 8th century. In summer there are live drama performances and craft displays.

Fårösund. Tel: (46) 498 22 10 18. Open: daily 11am–5pm. Admission charge.

Dalhem

Within a conservation area, **Gotlandståget** is an evocative steam-train journey on a 90-year-old locomotive covering a distance of 4km (2½ miles). It is the last operational stretch of the original Gotland Railway, which was inaugurated in 1878 by King Oscar II but was closed in its entirety in

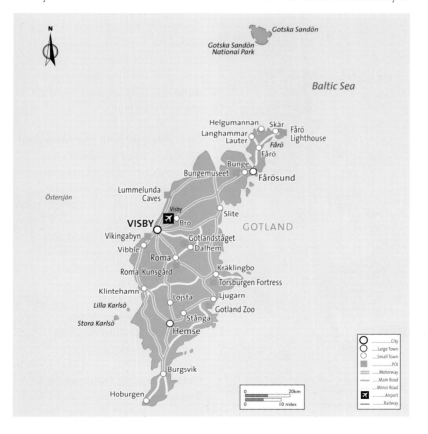

○	City
○	Large Town
○	Small Town
■	POI
	Motorway
	Main Road
	Minor Road
✈	Airport
	Railway

1960 with the advent of roads and motor traffic. At the Hesselby train station in Dalhem there is now a railway museum that preserves some of the former train coaches and other railway memorabilia, such as station masters' uniforms and railway tickets. *Tel: (46) 498 380 43. www. gotlandstaget.se/engelsk.htm. Train: Jun–Aug Wed–Thur, Sat 11am–4pm. Museum open: mid-Jun–mid-Aug daily 11am–4pm. Admission charge.*

Limestone stack at Fårö

Fårö

This tiny island, jutting off the northern tip of Gotland, is distinguished by pine forests and marshes and a long sand dune that attracts holidaymakers in summer. At one time fishing was the major occupation here, but this has largely given way to sheep farming, and today many of the former fishing huts, such as those at Helgumannen, have been converted into tourist accommodation. Traditional farmsteads, such as Lauter and Langhammar, are worth visiting for their 17th-century architecture. The limestone rocks just offshore have such mysterious shapes that locals have given them their own nicknames. Dominating the east coast is the Fårö Fyr (lighthouse), reaching a height of 30m (98ft).

Gotlands Djurpark (Gotland Zoo)

You feel as if you've stepped on to African soil at the island's zoo, where zebras, antelopes and camels, among other animals such as kangaroos, roam around their vast enclosures. Children will particularly love feeding time, when they can accompany the zookeepers in a horse and cart. *Guffride, Alskog. Tel: (46) 498 49 35 00. Open: mid-May–mid-Jun daily 10am–4pm; mid-Jun–Aug daily 10am–6pm. Admission charge.*

Gotska Sandön National Park

This isolated uninhabited island has been protected as a national park since

GOTLAND PONIES

The Gotland pony, known as *russ* in Sweden or more locally as *skogsbaggar* ('forest rams'), are known to have inhabited the island for thousands of years, evidenced in rock carvings depicting them. The ponies are thought to have descended from the wild Tarpan species, and are still considered wild animals rather than domesticated, grazing on the moors by Lojsta. By the 18th and 19th centuries the horses were used as draft animals in the agricultural industry and later in the mining industry to pull heavy equipment. As the island's forests began to be cultivated the horses lost more and more of their grazing land and became endangered. But with intervention from environmentalists an area was created for the ponies and the population began to increase again. These black or buckskin breeds are known to be stubborn by nature but are also strong trotters, good showjumpers and ideal for child riders.

area for its population of geese, larks, starlings and other species.

Karlsöarna (Karlsö Islands)

The Stora Karlsö area, 6km (4 miles) off the coast of Gotland, is now protected as a nature reserve for its large expanse of moorland and cliffs that are a breeding ground for a variety of orchids. Birdwatchers are also in their element, with a variety of gulls, razorbills and guillemots making their home here. A museum on the island details the history of habitation on the island since prehistoric times. Neighbouring Lilla Karlsö is also protected and is an important grazing ground for local Gotland sheep as well as a breeding site for peregrine falcons. There are regular boat trips from Gotland to these islands.

Ljugarn

A popular summer resort since the turn of the 20th century, Ljugarn particularly draws anglers with opportunities to catch pike, perch, salmon and flounder. The area is also good for cycling and walking. The main street is attractively lined with 19th-century buildings with characteristic yellow façades, while a traditional smoking house for fish can be seen at the harbour.

the early 20th century because of its sand dunes, pine forests and birdlife. The landscape almost entirely consists of sand, hence its name, and is home to a series of beetle species, hares and grey seals. Ferries sail to the island in summer from Fårö, weather permitting, and it is possible to camp on the island overnight for a true nature experience.

Hoburgen

This cliff area is best known for the limestone stack called the 'Old Man of Hoburg'. The rock formation resembles a man's face and long nose looking out to sea. It's also a popular birdwatching

Lojsta

The most important sight in Lojsta is the medieval church, which contains an original choir and nave and stained-glass windows. The figures over the chancel, depicting Christ surrounded by saints Peter, Paul, Michael and Margaret, were painted around 1350 by an artist known as Egypticus, while the paintings on the northern and southern walls date from the 15th and 16th centuries respectively. Nearby, the Lojsta Hed forest area is home to the distinctive local ponies.

Lummelundagrottorna (Lummelunda Caves)

These caves were discovered by two curious boys in 1948. Within these underground grottoes, which are among the most popular sights on the island, are stalactites, stalagmites and beautiful water features. Guided tours are available.

Tel: (46) 498 27 30 50. Open: May–mid-Jun & mid-Aug–mid-Sept daily 10am–2pm; mid-Jun–mid-Aug daily 9am–6pm.
Admission charge.

Roma Kungsgård

In the 12th century a group of Cistercian monks from Nydala on the mainland founded a monastery here. The monastery became of great importance and thrived until the Reformation in 1530. It subsequently turned to ruin, but stones from the former religious centre were used to

The medieval wall around Visby

construct the Roma Kungsgård, the home of the county governor. All that remains of the original monastery today are the transept, a choir and the northern chapel. The site is popular as a setting for Shakespeare in summer.
Tel: (46) 498 290 353. Open: May Sat & Sun 10am–5pm; Jun–Sept daily 10am–6pm. Admission charge.

Stånga

Not far from Lojsta, in the town of Stånga, takes place one of the most unique annual events on the island – the Stånga Games. More than 2,000 participants compete during the second week of July in ancient sports, many of which date back to Viking times, such as stone-pole throwing (similar to tossing the caber in Scotland), square-and-border-ball (similar to French boules) and a pentathlon. Originally the games were a friendly contest between the people of neighbouring villages and were revived as a major sporting event in 1924. They went annual in the 1960s.

Torsburgen Fortress

Dating from the 4th century, this impressive fortress is protected by a 7m (23ft) high wall. It is the largest prehistoric defence structure in Sweden, with the oldest part having been built in the Iron Age.
Kräklingbo. Open: daily. Free admission.

Visby

Surrounded by a 3.5m (11ft) medieval wall built as a defence with 40 towers, the centre of Visby is now protected by UNESCO as a World Heritage Site. With its vaulted streets paved with cobblestones, it is one of the most authentic and charming cities in the country. Outside the city walls are a bustling harbour and a pretty park. Visby's history goes back to Viking times, but it was during the 13th century, when the town began to trade with the German Hanseatic League, that things really took off. By 1361, however, the town fell to Danish control and was not returned to Sweden until the 17th century.

Bötaniska Trädgården (Botanical Gardens)

Founded in 1855, a herb garden and a rose garden are just two of the attractions in the city's botanical gardens, besides a pretty lily pond. A number of species not native to the area can also be found here, such as mulberry and walnut, and some Oriental plants and trees. The ruins of the 13th-century St Olav's church are also set within the gardens.
St Nikolaigatan 11. Tel: (46) 498 26 94 77. Open: daily. Free admission.

Domkyrkan Sankta Maria (St Mary's Cathedral)

The only church in Visby dating from medieval times that is completely intact, much of the current appearance

Helge And church

is Gothic in style thanks to additions made in the 14th century. The Gothic southern chapel was renovated in the Baroque style during the 18th century, at the same time as the spires were added, but restored to its original appearance during renovation in 1901. The baptismal font and the statue of Christ are original, while the beautifully carved pulpit dates from 1684.
Våstra Kyrkogatan 5. Tel: (46) 498 20 68 12. Open: daily. Free admission.

Gotland Historical Museum

Newly opened in 2007, the most impressive collection in the island's Historical Museum is its silverware, dating from Viking times to the 19th century. There's also a science centre with plenty of hands-on exhibits.
Strandgatan 14 (Visby). Tel: (46) 498 29 27 00. Open: mid-Apr–mid-Sept daily 10am–5pm; mid-Sept–mid-Apr Tue–Sun noon–4pm. Admission charge.

Gotlands Länsmuseet (Gotlands County Museum)

There are three main areas that comprise the Gotlands County Museum, focusing on history, art and science in the area. The Gotlands Fornsal (Historical Museum) on Strandgatan uncovers all aspects of the island's 8,000-year history, and, unsurprisingly, given the wealth of treasures found here, centres largely on the hoards from the Viking era. The Gotlands Konstmuseet (Art Museum) is housed in an attractive 19th-century building at Hansgatan 21 and displays artworks by both local and international artists. The Fenomenalen (Science Centre), also on Strandgatan, explores all manner of scientific activity and natural history.
Strandgatan 14. Tel: (46) 498 29 27 00. www.lansmuseetgotland.se. Open: mid-Jun–mid-Sept daily 10am–6pm; mid-Sept–mid-Jun daily noon–4pm. Admission charge.

Helge And (Church of the Holy Spirit)

Another of the town's 13th-century churches, this was used for the care of the sick and poor, and its former

octagonal form can still be discerned despite the ruined condition.
Hospitalsgatan. Tel: (46) 498 29 27 00. Open: daily. Free admission.

Kapitelhusgården

The centre of Visby's famous Medieval Week (*see p27*) is this bustling courtyard dating from the 12th century. Visitors can attempt medieval crafts such as spinning wool and eat traditional medieval food such as mutton and beer. There's also an exhibition detailing the island's capture by the Danes in 1361.
Drottensgatan 8. Tel: (46) 498 24 76 37. Open: Jun–Sept daily. Free admission.

Langska Huset

The former home of the 18th-century textile master Tobias Langska is today a handicrafts centre devoted to the island's many craft traditions. As well as exhibits and lectures, visitors are welcome to embark on training sessions to learn the skills for themselves.
Kopparsviksgatan 7. Tel: (46) 498 21 71 60. Open: Tue–Thur 9am–4pm. Admission charge.

St Nicolai

A former Dominican monastery, now in ruins, St Nicolai was dedicated to the patron saint of sailors but was destroyed, like so many of the town's churches, in the 16th century. Today it forms a backdrop for concerts and dramatic performances including an annual chamber music festival.
Odalgatan. Tel: (46) 498 29 27 00. Open: daily. Free admission.

Stora Torget

Visby's main square is the focal point of the town and is surrounded by lovely gabled buildings from the Middle Ages, many of which have now been converted into atmospheric restaurants. The Franciscan church of St Karin (St Catherine) on the south side of the square was built in 1233 but destroyed during the 16th-century Reformation. It is now a ruin, but there is an exhibition in the cloisters.

Vikingabyn (Viking Village)

Because of its strategic location in the middle of the Baltic Sea, Gotland was a highly important trading centre during the Viking era, bridging the gap between Scandinavia and Northern Europe. This Viking Village re-creates life as it would have been then, with longhouses, flour mills and competitive sports. Guides dress up in full Viking regalia, and visitors can try their hand at tossing the caber, a traditional Viking pastime. There are also museum exhibits displaying the vast array of archaeological finds from the island, including the largest discovery of silver jewellery.
Tofta Strand. Tel: (46) 498 29 71 00. www.vikingabyn.se. Open: July–mid-Aug Tue–Sat 11am–5pm. Admission charge.

The Vikings

Most people imagine the half-legendary Vikings of Scandinavia to be bloodthirsty, warlike relics of the Dark Ages. That image was fostered by the Christian Church, whose wealthy, defenceless abbeys and monasteries – often on remote North Sea islands – were easy prey for Viking longships, and it was perpetuated by a cycle of Hollywood movies, usually wildly imaginative and historically inaccurate.

The name 'Viking' comes from the Swedish word for a bay or inlet of the sea, 'vik'. While the 'vikings' of the Danish and Norwegian coasts headed west in search of land and loot,

Part of a Viking village at Höllriken

ravaging and settling the shores of England, Scotland, Ireland and northern France, the Swedish Vikings headed east, across the Baltic and up the river Neva to Ladoga, then onward along the rivers of present-day Russia as far as Constantinople and the Islamic world.

These early merchant adventurers went not in search of land or loot but in pursuit of trade – although they were fierce fighters when needed, and not averse to turning to the sword if peaceful commerce proved difficult or unprofitable.

In Constantinople, which the Swedes called 'Miklagard' (Great City), the Byzantine emperors valued the loyalty and fighting ability of Swedish (and other) Vikings so highly that they were recruited into the Varangir Guard, and many Vikings, perhaps more hot-headed than their commercially minded cousins, travelled from Scandinavia specifically to lend their services as imperial bodyguards.

The Swedish voyagers and settlers even lent their name to modern Russia: the Slavic people of the region called the Swedes 'Rus' or 'redheads'.

Archaeological finds show that there was much trade between

Inside the Viking fortress at Trelleborg

Sweden and the eastern Mediterranean and the Black Sea region, and on the banks of the Volga Swedish merchant princes founded a settlement called Holmgard which grew eventually into the powerful principality of Novgorod. Swedish Vikings also settled Kiev, destined to be another of Muscovy's great cities, and the descendants of Viking dynasties still ruled parts of Russia as semi-independent princes until the 17th century.

The island of Gotland was one of the main centres of Viking trade, and from their own accounts and from archaeological evidence we know that Gotland traders travelled across the known world, to Jerusalem (which they called Jorsalir), the Caspian Sea and Baghdad (which they knew as Särkland). Traders and mercenary warriors returning to Gotland brought back treasure from all these places, and more medieval silver coins minted in the Caliphate of Baghdad have been unearthed in Gotland than in all the rest of Europe.

Birka, on Bjorko Island near modern Stockholm, was another wealthy settlement of Viking traders, with a population of about 2,000 people – a major city in the 9th century.

At the beginning of the Viking era, around AD 750, Sweden was divided into hundreds of small chiefdoms, often comprising no more than one extended ruling family and its thralls (slaves) and dependants. These Viking mini-kingdoms gradually merged over the next three centuries to become a united Swedish state.

Svealand

The Svealand region at the heart of Sweden is a pastoral idyll of lakes and mountains, castles and wooden huts, all enhanced by a slow and calming pace of life. Much of the area owes its prosperity to mining, which has contributed greatly to the wealth of the entire country. It has also been a breeding ground for some of the country's most prominent figures, from the scientific genius of Carl von Linné to the artistic skills of Carl Larsson, the latter's work defining Swedish country life.

EASTERN SVEALAND

Älvkarleby

Set within the Dalälven river delta, the dominant sight in Älvkarleby is its hydroelectric power station, but the area is also hugely popular with fishermen because of its large population of salmon. It's claimed that more salmon and trout are caught in the rapids here than in any other part of Scandinavia. There's also an 18-hole golf course, with the added incentive of breathtaking views while you're aiming for your hole in one.

Birka

Generally thought to be the country's oldest town, Birka, on the island of Björkö, was established in the 8th century as a trading post and became the launching site for many Viking voyages. It was also one of the first places in Sweden to adopt Christianity. Today ancient burial mounds can be seen, and visitors can also watch the archaeological digs that are constantly going on.

Engelsberg Bruk

Preservation of the early stages of industrialisation is today considered as important as the conservation of architectural gems. As a result, the ironworks in the town of Engelsberg have now been designated a UNESCO World Heritage Site. The blast furnace dates from the late 18th century and has been preserved in pristine condition, as have the smelting houses, workers' homes and offices and the mine owner's mansion.

Fagersta. Tel: (46) 220 243 05. www.ekomuseum.se. Open for tours mid-May–mid-Jun Sat & Sun 10am & 1pm; mid-Jun–mid-Aug daily 10am, 1pm & 3pm. Admission charge.

Gävle

Much of Gävle was destroyed by fire at the end of the 18th century, and only its town hall survived the blaze in the city centre, but today it is an attractive place made up of 19th-century architecture. The Old Town area

(Gamle Gefle), however, managed to preserve its earlier buildings. One of the quirks of Gävle is its giant Christmas goat, built of straw and put up in the town's square for the festive season. Its infamy, however, is due to the habit of local youths of trying to burn it down each year.

Sveriges Järnvägsmuseum (National Railway Museum)

Gävle's most popular attraction is the National Railway Museum, displaying a wide range of trains and locomotives through the ages.

Rälsgatan 1. Tel: (46) 026 14 46 15. Open: Jun–Aug 10am–4pm daily; Sept–May Tue–Sun 10am–4pm. Admission charge.

Gripsholms Slott

Once the royal residence of King Gustav III, Gripsholms Castle in Mariefred is now home to the Swedish National Portrait Gallery, with more than 4,000 permanent artworks and a changing programme of temporary

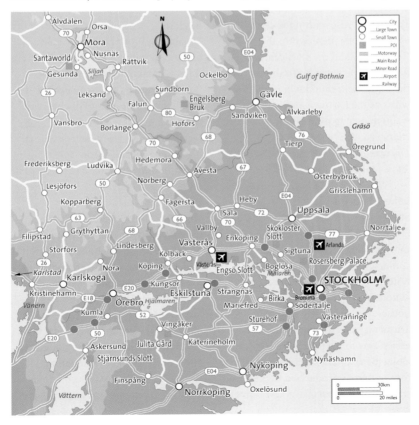

An old locomotive at the National Railway Museum in Gävle

exhibitions. Also within the castle are various rooms preserved in the Renaissance and the 18th-century Baroque style, including a theatre. In the town itself, children in particular will love the narrow-gauge stream trains that chug through it.
Mariefred. Tel: (46) 159 101 94. Open: mid-May–mid-Sept daily 10am–4pm. Admission charge.

Lake Mälaren

Stretching westward from the capital Stockholm, Lake Mälaren is one of the most enchanting bodies of water in the country. Its numerous fingers of waterways and islands boast an abundance of grand castles and manor houses used by royalty and the aristocracy over the centuries. The easiest way to see the castles is by car along the road that circles the area, but for the finest introduction to the grand waterfront façades, take an evocative cruise along the lake.

Boglösa

Fascinating Bronze Age rock carvings have been found in this town, depicting ships, animals and hunting. Inside Boglösa Church there is an exhibit detailing the history and discovery of the carvings.
Open: Jun & Aug–mid-Sept Sat & Sun noon–5pm; Jul daily noon–5pm. Free admission.

Engsö Slott

One of the most interesting castles in the area is Engsö, reputedly haunted. The stone house was built in the 15th century but considerably renovated in the 1740s. Inside, individual rooms evoke different eras of the house's history. At Christmas the castle's craft market in the grounds is popular with locals from all around. The castle also offers overnight accommodation.
Engsö. Tel: (46) 171 44 40 12. www.engsoslott.com. Open: May, Jun & mid–end Aug Sat & Sun noon–5pm;

July–mid-Aug Sat–Thur noon–5pm. Admission charge.

Grönsöö Slott

Another spectacular castle lining the lake, Grönsöö was built in 1611 in the French Renaissance style. However, it was completely renovated in the 18th century in the Baroque style and this is the grand decoration that fills the rooms today. Next to the castle is a most unusual sight – a Chinese pavilion decorated with seashells. Within the grounds there are grand avenues, an orchard that includes a lime tree planted in the 1620s, and perennial flower gardens.

Enköping. Tel: (46) 171 870 84. www.gronsoo.se. Open for tours mid-May–mid-Sept Sat & Sun 1pm. Admission charge.

Lake Mälaren

Rosersberg Palace

Originally built in the Renaissance style, Rosersberg has been renovated and altered many times over the centuries. In the early 19th century it became the summer residence of the royal family and some of the finest rooms date from this period, including King Karl XIV's opulent bedroom.

Rosersberg. Tel: (46) 859 03 50 39. Open: by appointment. Admission charge.

Skokloster Slott

Built in the 17th century, this stunning Baroque castle with its striking domed turrets contains a vast collection of antique furniture, weaponry and armoury, while next door there is an automobile museum displaying vintage

A cruise is the best way to experience Lake Mälaren

The symmetrical Strömsholm Palace

cars. Surrounding the castle is a beautiful landscaped park.
Skokloster. Tel: (46) 84 02 30 60.
www.skoklostersslott.se.
Open: Apr Sat & Sun 11.30am–4.30pm;
May Tue–Sun 11.30am–4.30pm;
Jun–Aug Tue–Sun 11.30am–5.30pm;
Sept Tue–Fri 12.30pm–4.30pm, Sat &
Sun 11.30am–4.30pm; Oct Sat & Sun
11.30am–4.30pm. Admission charge.

Steninge Slott

Just outside Sigtuna, Sweden's second-oldest town after Birka, is this truly magnificent palace with breathtakingly ornate rooms, including a gilt and leather room, a grand staircase and well-preserved frescoes and friezes. In the grounds there is a distinctive octagonal bell tower. Although the site dates back to the 13th century, it was the period between 1650 and 1850 that saw the most influence on the palace. The other attraction, particularly for families, is the

cultural centre where you can try your hand at traditional Swedish crafts such as glass-blowing and candle-making.
Stenlagugården, Märsta.
Tel: (46) 859 25 95 00.
www.steningeslott.com.
Open: Palace tours Sat & Sun 1pm,
2.30pm & 4pm; Cultural Centre
Mon–Fri 11am–5pm, Sat & Sun
10am–5pm. Admission charge.

Strömsholm Palace

The distinctive yellow façade of Strömsholm is dominated by a central tower and four corner towers. Among the internal features are a sumptuous Chinese-style dining room and the bedroom that was used by Princess Sofia Magdalena in the 18th century. From 1868 to 1968 the palace was home to the Swedish Army Riding School and had a stud farm in the grounds. There is still a riding school here for gifted young equestrians.

Kolbäck. Tel: (46) 220 43 035.
Open: May Sat & Sun noon–4pm; Jun &
Aug daily noon–4pm; July daily
noon–5pm. Admission charge.

Tel: (46) 213 98 070.
www.vallbyfriluftsmuseum.se.
Open: daily 10am–5pm.
Free admission.

Sturehof

The most distinctive feature of this
18th-century manor house is the
collection of tiled stoves, from the
porcelain factory owned by the house's
one-time resident. While far less grand
than many other houses in the area, the
grounds make for a pleasant stroll.
Tel: (46) 853 02 82 40. Open: May–Sept
Sun 1–3pm. Admission charge.

Vallby Friluftsmuseum

On the outskirts of Västerås is this
open-air museum that preserves several
wooden country homes from around
the region. The museum is patrolled
by costumed guides, and children
in particular will love petting the
farm animals. There are also various
craft demonstrations.

Västerås

Västerås has been an important town
since Viking times, and just outside the
town centre is the burial mound of
what is thought to be the Viking Bröt
Anund. The most important building
in this city is the cathedral, which
contains the tomb of the unfortunate
King Erik XIV (*see p131*).

Nyköpinghus

Nyköping is well known in Swedish
history as the site of the infamous
Nyköping Banquet, when King Birger
invited his two brothers to dine with
him. After the meal the two brothers
went to bed but were woken up by
the king's subordinates and locked
in the dungeon. The king threw the
key into the river, leaving his brothers

The harbour at Västerås

to starve to death, but his actions resulted in a people's riot and Birger was banished. The next period of note was during the 15th century when the future King Karl IX renovated the castle in impressive Renaissance style. Much of the original castle, however, was destroyed by fire in 1665. The banquet is commemorated every year with a parade, and in summer a floral representation of the fateful key blooms on the riverbank. Inside the castle are two exhibitions detailing the building's two periods of importance.

Tel: (46) 155 24 57 00.
Open: mid-Aug–mid-Jun Tue–Sun 11am–4pm; mid-Jun–mid-Aug daily 11am–4pm. Admission charge.

Öregrund

Öregrund was devastated by a fire started by invading Russians in the early 18th century, but unlike many other towns around the country that suffered a similar fate, the town was rebuilt in wood according to its previous appearance. The town's church includes a 15th-century altar that survived the blaze and two votive ships in the nave. The heart of Öregrund, however, is the harbour region with its abundance of restaurants and cafés. Offshore, the Öregrund archipelago features a number of islands where there is a variety of summer activities on offer, such as boating and fishing.

Österbybruk

The town's castle was the scene of the imprisonment and alleged assassination of King Erik XIV in 1577. Although the truth about his death has never been proved, it is thought that he was served soup laced with arsenic at the order of his brother because he had become mentally ill. He is buried in Västerås cathedral (*see p119*). The town was also the centre of the region's iron industry, which is commemorated today with a sound-and-light show performed by puppets in the former forge. The now defunct mine is open to visitors.

Sala

Sala came to prominence in the 16th century when silver was discovered here and the mines were a profitable part of the local economy for centuries. Also of note in the town are its two picturesque churches.

Sala Silvergruva

Tours to the old silver mine take visitors down to a depth of 60m (197ft) to explore the former pits that were operational for more than 400 years until they closed in 1908. Torches and rubber boots to cope with the dark and slippery surfaces are supplied. For those who don't want to make this rather eerie trip there are plenty of above-ground exhibits that tell the history of the mine and the miners' lives.
Drottning Christinas Väg.
Tel: (46) 224 677 250.

www.salasilvergruva.se. Open: Oct–Apr daily 11am–4pm; May–Sept daily 10am–5pm. Admission charge.

Strängnäs

Gyllenhjelmsgatan is considered by many to be the most attractive street in the entire country, offering a classic Swedish landscape of red-painted clapboard houses along a narrow winding lane. The most important event in the town's history was the election of Gustav Vasa (*see p13*) as king on 6 June 1523 in Strängnäs's cathedral. The day is celebrated every year as Sweden's National Day.

Uppsala

Often referred to as the 'birthplace of Sweden', Uppsala is today one of the country's major cities and renowned as the site of the country's first university, established in 1477. One of its most impressive buildings is its medieval Gothic cathedral (Domkyrkan), with tall spires dominating the landscape. Inside are the burial tombs of King Gustav Vasa and the remains of St Erik, the national patron saint.

Botaniska Trädgården

Thanks to the influence of Carl von Linné, Uppsala's botanical gardens became one of the most famous and important in the world. They are also the oldest in Sweden, founded in 1655. Today the gardens cover 14ha (34 acres) including an orangery, a tropical greenhouse, research gardens and rock gardens. *Villavägen 8. Tel: (46) 18 471 28 38. www.botan.uu.se. Open: May–Sept daily 7am–9pm; Oct–Apr daily 7am–7pm. Admission charge to the greenhouse.*

Strängnäs and its cathedral

Gamla Uppsala's church bell tower

Carolinabiblioteket
(Carolina Rediviva Library)

Founded in 1620, the university's main library now contains more than five million books and an equally impressive array of manuscripts. The most famous item here is the 6th-century Silver Bible.

Dag Hammarskjöldsväg 1.
Tel: (46) 18 471 39 00. www.ub.uu.se.
Open: mid-Jun–mid-Aug Mon–Fri 9am–5pm, Sat 10am–5pm (mid-May–Aug Sun 11am–4pm); mid-Aug–mid-Jun Mon–Fri 9am–8pm, Sat 10am–5pm. Admission charge mid-May–Sept.

Gamla Uppsala

'Old Uppsala' just north of the city centre is generally considered to be the site of the emergence of 'modern' Sweden. Before the advent of Christianity this was a pagan worshipping site, and there are several 6th-century burial mounds here, but a church was eventually built in the area, which was used for Swedish coronations until the ceremony moved to the cathedral in the city proper. For a greater understanding of this important area, visit the museum that details the history and development of the city and the country, as well as the many myths that surround it.

Museum Disavägen. Tel: (46) 18 23 93 00. www.raa.se/gamlauppsala.
Open: Jan–Apr Wed, Sat & Sun 12–3pm; May–Aug daily 11am–5pm; Sept daily 11–4pm; Oct–Nov Mon, Wed, Sat & Sun noon–3pm. Admission charge.

Linnaeus Museum

The former home of Carl von Linné is now a museum dedicated to this great man, and includes his library, study, cabinets of insects and herbs, original

18th-century furnishings and details of his work. There's also a real sense of family life here, with linen tablecloths, wineglasses and even his daughter's wedding dress on display.
Svartbäcksgatan 27.
Tel: (46) 18 131 65 40. Open: May–mid-Sept daily 11am–5pm. Admission charge.

Universitethuset (University Hall)
Although the city's university dates back to the Middle Ages, its main building was built in the 19th century. The building currently houses the majority of the university's art collection, which can be viewed as part of a guided tour.
St Olafsgatan. Tel: (46) 18 471 17 15.
Open: Mon–Fri 8am–4pm.
Free admission.

Uppland Museum
Set in an 18th-century mill, the county museum explores the history of the province. It's a great place to come for an overall view of local crafts, folk traditions and the Viking heritage.
St Eriks Torg 10. Tel: (46) 18 16 91 00.
Open: Tue–Sun noon–5pm.
Admission charge.

Uppsala Slott
The city's castle as seen today is largely the result of rebuilding in the 18th century after the original 16th-century building was destroyed by fire. Today it contains the *Riksalen* (Hall of State), an art museum and a waxworks collection of figures dressed in historical costumes.

The Gothic cathedral at Uppsala

Burial mounds dating from the 6th century in Gamla Uppsala

Slottsbacken. Tel: (46) 18 54 48 11.
Open: Tours mid-Jun–Aug Tue–Sun
1pm & 3pm. Admission charge.

WESTERN SVEALAND
Askersund

The most prominent building in
Askersund is the Landskyrkan, a
beautifully designed 17th-century
church, but it is the town's setting on
the tranquil Lake Vättern that is the
real draw, especially in summer. Just
outside town is the Stjärnsunds Slott, a
former royal residence decorated with
elegant 19th-century furnishings.

Falun

Falun was a centre of the region's
mining industry, and its importance to
the country has earned it World
Heritage status.

Dalarna Museum

This museum features the library of
Sweden's acclaimed writer Selma
Lagerlöf, as well as various collections of
folk art and folk costumes.
Tel: (46) 23 76 55 00.
Open: Mon–Fri 10am–5pm, Sat & Sun
noon–5pm. Admission charge.

Store Kopparberget

The Store Kopparberget mine and its
adjoining museum offer a fascinating
insight into the workings of the mine
and the lives of the mining community,
including preserved miners' cottages.
The real claim to fame is the red paint
that was produced from the iron
sulphate mined here which adorns
a large number of the buildings in
Sweden. Visitors can descend 55m
(180ft) to the pits to learn about the

history of the industry and gain a greater understanding of the sheer hard labour involved.
Tel: (46) 23 78 20 30.
www.kopparberget.com. Open: Jun & Aug–Sept Mon–Fri 10am–4pm, Sat & Sun 11am–3pm; July daily 10am–5pm. Free admission.

Filipstad

Filipstad, like much of the Svealand region, owes its prosperity largely to mining, and various former pits can be visited. It is also noted as the childhood home of the great 20th-century Swedish poet Nils Ferlin, who is commemorated by a statue sitting on a park bench in the centre of town. Today, the town is best known for its Wasabröd factory, the producers of that great Swedish mainstay, crispbread.

Grythyttan

Today Grythyttan is best known as a gastronomic centre for traditional Swedish cuisine with a popular cooking school, and annual awards for the world's best cookbooks. The town, however, has been important since the 17th century, particularly for its spa at the nearby Loka Brun. The spa is completely modern now, but former facilities such as the bathhouse and kitchen can still be seen in an adjoining museum.

Hedemora

This pretty wooden town dates back to the Middle Ages, although, as in so much of Sweden, most of the current buildings were constructed after a fire in the 19th century. One of the most important buildings in town is the lakeside Hedemora Gammelgård, one of the oldest-surviving homesteads in the country.

Theaterladen (Theatre Barn)

Set in a converted early 19th-century granary is one of Sweden's most unusual theatres, with summer performances staged in the manner of Victorian drama by local amateur groups. There's also a small theatre museum on the site detailing Swedish provincial theatre.
Gussavasgatan 10. Tel: (46) 225 151 15. Open: mid-May–Sept daily. Admission charge.

CARL VON LINNÉ

The way in which we now refer to every plant and animal by two Latin words, known as the biological name, and the science of taxonomy are almost entirely due to the work of the botanist Carl von Linné (1707–78), who was a professor at Uppsala University. Also known as Carolus Linnaeus, he published the *Systema Naturae* in 1735, which simplified the previously unwieldy naming of every creation of nature according to the hierarchy of its genus and species. He also applied a common-sense approach for ease of reference: mammals (*mammalia*), for example, were named for their mammary glands. Less favourably, however, he also defined race into four categories according to place of birth and skin colour and added characteristics to each that in today's light seem highly prejudiced. In his honour, his home province of Småland now has the *Linnaea borealis* as its official flower.

Drive: Fryken Lake

The shimmering waters of Fryken Lake, surrounded by forests and lined with elegant mansions, make for an ideal day's drive, covering approximately 40km (25 miles). Alternatively, the area can be seen via the 19th-century steamer that plies the waters or via the Fryksdalsbanan, which has been dubbed the most beautiful train journey in the country.

This route covers 70km (43 miles), so allow a full day.

Start at the southern end of the lake at the town of Kil and follow the signposts north to Östra Ämtervik and Minnesgård.

1 Mårbacka

This former home of the Nobel Prize-winning author Selma Lagerlöf (*see pp22–3*) has been preserved as it was when she lived here until her death in 1940. Many of her personal possessions, such as her writing desk, can be seen, and there are detailed exhibitions on her life and work. Among her most acclaimed novels is *The Wonderful Adventures of Nils*. *Continue north and cross the road bridge over the lake on to road No 45. Turn left southwards to Rottneros.*

2 Rottneros Park

This beautiful colonnaded mansion was the setting for the fictional Ekeby in Selma Lagerlöf's novel *Gösta Berling's Saga* and today is open to the public, as are the stunning landscaped gardens and sculpture park. There's also a children's adventure park to keep the little ones entertained and an exhibition of vintage motorcycles. *Return north along road No 45 to Sunne.*

3 Sunne

The main centre of the region makes for a pleasant stop-off. At the Sunne Hembygdsgård various buildings have been preserved, including a former schoolhouse, a general store and a courthouse.

Mårbacka
Mårbackastiftelsen, Minnesgård. Tel: (46) 565 310 27. www.marbacka.com. Open: May & Sept Sat & Sun 11am–3pm; Jun daily 11am–4pm; July–mid-Aug daily 10am–5pm; mid–end Aug daily 11am–4pm; Oct–Dec Sat 2pm. Admission charge.

Rottneros Park
Tel: (46) 565 602 95. Open: mid-May–mid-Jun & mid-Aug–mid-Sept daily 10am–4pm; mid-Jun–mid-Aug daily 10am–6pm. Admission charge.

Torsby
Utterbyn 49. Tel: (46) 560 100 26. www.varmland.org/torsby. Open: mid-Jun–mid-Aug. Call for times. Admission charge.

Continue north along road No 45 for about 35km (22 miles) to Torsby.

4 Torsby

Sahlströmska Gården was the home of two sibling artists and now displays an eclectic collection of 20th-century Swedish paintings. Also in town is a museum of vintage cars and a Finnish Cultural Centre that pays tribute to the Finnish immigrants who lived in the region (when the two countries were one) to work in the forestry industry.

Torsby in winter

Drive: Fryken Lake

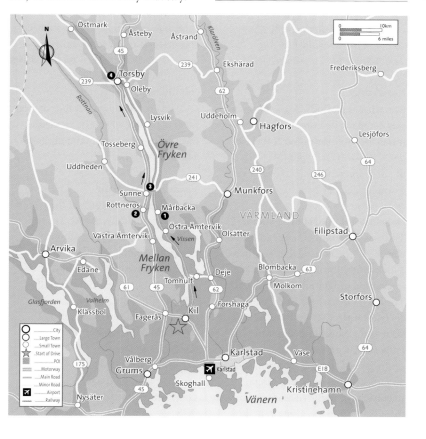

Julita Gård

The largest open-air museum in the world is also a working farm and a breeding site for endangered animals. During the medieval period the estate was the site of a monastery, and later became a royal residence, but was turned into a cultural museum in the 1940s. Among the exhibits are farmers' homesteads, a fire station, church, herb garden and orchards, all showcasing agricultural life in the early 20th century.
Julita. Tel: (46) 150 48 75 00.
www.nordiskamuseet.se/julita.
Open: May–mid-Jun & Sept
daily 11am–4pm; mid-Jun–Aug
daily 10am–6pm. Admission charge.

Karlskoga

Ever since the Middle Ages, this area was noted for its iron ore deposits, but it was the inventor Alfred Nobel (*see pp132–3*) who really put this town on the map when he came to own a vast weaponry factory here.

Nobelmuseet, Björkborns Manor

This was the summer home of Alfred Nobel and the house, with its original 19th-century furnishings, offers a fascinating insight into life at the time. The laboratory where Nobel worked is also now open to the public. Next door to the Nobel Museum is the Fiffiga Huset, an experimental science centre geared towards children, and an industrial museum explaining the history of industrialisation throughout Sweden.

Tel: (46) 586 834 94.
Open: Jun–Aug Tue–Sun 11am–4pm;
Sept–May by appointment.
Admission charge.

Karlstad

Named after the 16th-century king Karl IX, many of Karlstad's original buildings were destroyed by fire, but on Västra Älvgrenen the few wooden buildings that did survive have been kept together within a cultural centre. The town's former prison on Karlsbergsgatan, which closed down in 1968, has, rather incongruously, been converted into a hotel, but the basement cells have been preserved as a museum detailing the lives and conditions of the prisoners who were once incarcerated here. In the centre of town is a statue of one of Sweden's most beloved authors, Selma Lagerlöf, who was born nearby.

Värmlands Museum

History and folk culture of the region going as far back as the Ice Age is the focus at this award-winning museum. Among the permanent exhibitions are details about the world-famous linen industry and other textiles, the salmon fishing industry and forestry, as well as a collection of artworks.
Sandgrundsudden.
Tel: (46) 54 701 19 00.
www.varmlandsmuseum.se.
Open: daily 10am–5pm.
Admission charge.

Leksand

Leksand is best known for its Midsummer Festival (*see p26*) which is the most popular in the country. Surrounding the town's 13th-century church there are also a number of preserved wooden cottages that now constitute the town's heritage centre. A cultural centre also displays many items of local art and folk costumes.

Mora

Mora is best known as the finishing line of the Vasaloppet ski race (*see p26*). The race is held every year in March in memory of the 90km (56-mile) run undertaken by Gustav Vasa after he heard news of the Stockholm Bloodbath (*see p13*), and a statue of the great man stands at the finishing post. There's also a museum in town, the Vasaloppet Hus, which details the history of Vasa's journey and of the race.

Zorngården

The artist Anders Zorn (1860–1920) was a keen exponent of Sweden's National Romanticism movement, and his former home has now been preserved in the manner in which he lived, including a vast billiards room. Much of the furniture was built to Zorn's own design, inspired by the simplicity of country elements. The adjoining museum displays many of Zorn's works of art including some of his famous nudes, as well as a silver collection acquired by Zorn over the years.

Leksand church

Vasagatan 36. Tel: (46) 250 59 23 10.
Zorngården open: mid-May–mid-Sept
Mon–Sat 10am–4pm, Sun 11am–4pm;
mid-Sept–mid-May Mon–Sat
noon–4pm, Sun 1–4pm.
Zornmuseet open: mid-May–mid-Sept
Mon–Sat 9am–5pm, Sun 11am–5pm;
mid-Sept–mid-May Mon–Sat
noon–4pm, Sun 1–4pm.
Admission charge.

Nusnäs

The red-painted wooden horses that make such popular souvenirs from Sweden are produced in quantity in the town of Nusnäs. The history of the horses, known as Dalecarlian horses, is thought to go back to the 18th century when peasant men would pass away the cold winter nights carving them as toys for local children. They were painted with floral motifs similar to those used to decorate homes and churches. Today they are still carved by hand from a block of pine wood, painted individually, then exported all over the world.

Nils Olsson Hemslöjd

At one of the oldest manufacturers in Nusnäs, visitors can watch the craftspeople carving and decorating these distinctive pieces, seeing the process through from a single block of wood to the finished article. Clogs and clocks are also produced in abundance. *Tel: (46) 250 372 00.*

Open: mid-Jun–mid-Aug Mon–Fri 8am–6pm, Sat & Sun 9am–5pm; mid-Aug–mid-Jun Mon–Fri 8am–5pm, Sat 10am–2pm. Admission charge.

Nusnäs is famous for its red wooden horses

Svampen

The other great symbol of Nusnäs is this mushroom-shaped water tower built in the 1950s. Inside is a science exhibition, where visitors can conduct all kinds of water experiments, but its main attraction is the great views of the town and the surrounding area. *Dalbygatan 4. Tel: (46) 19 611 37 35. Open: May–Sept daily 11am–4pm. Admission charge.*

Wadköping

Following the riverside walkway from the castle leads to this charming open-air centre of old wooden houses relocated from other parts of the city. Most have now been converted into craft workshops, boutique shops and cafés. Among the buildings which are now a museum is the **Kungsstugan**, named after King Karl IX who stayed here, and where visitors can admire frescoes from the late 16th century. The area is particularly evocative in summer when concerts and plays are staged here. *Tel: (46) 19 21 62 20. Open: Tue–Sun 11am–5pm. Free admission.*

Örebro

The most famous sight in Örebro and one of the most renowned in the country is the castle (*slott*) standing majestically on the banks of the river. It was here, among other things, that the Swedes elected the Frenchman Jean Baptiste Bernadotte to ascend the Swedish throne. The town's tourist office is also located within the castle.

Orsa

Traditionally an agricultural area, particularly for the production of cheese and other dairy produce, the Orsa region is now a popular tourist area for outdoor activities such as horse riding and hiking. It is also a centre for basket weaving. Just north of Orsa is **Grönklitt**, an enclosed nature park where visitors can observe bears, wolves and other native but fearsome animals at close range. Breeding programmes take place regularly, so if you're lucky you'll see bear cubs and other young.

Grönklitt: Tel: (46) 250 462 00.
Open: mid-May–Jun & mid-Aug–mid-Sept daily 10am–3pm; July–mid-Aug daily 10am–6pm. Admission charge.

Rättvik

For a sense of the speed and excitement experienced by professional bobsleighers, take the wheeled toboggan run here, the Sommer Rodel. Rättvik is popular year-round, for skiing in winter and sailing in summer. Just outside town, in Dalhalla, opera comes to life at the amphitheatre converted from a former quarry and renowned for its acoustics. Aside from opera performances, daily tours can be made to the quarry in summer to learn about its geological and man-made history.

Sundborn

Sweden's beloved artist Carl Larsson (*see p23*) lived in this town, and his former home, **Carl Larssongården**, is now a museum devoted to his work.

Wandering around the house it's easy to understand the convivial life of Larsson, his wife and their six children that made them such favourites, from the cheery dining room in primary colours, the summery living room, to the comforting bedrooms. Traditional wooden furniture and other features of early 20th-century design are on display. One of Larsson's most famous works was *Ett Hem* (*At Home*) depicting his family's life here, so it is no surprise that this is one of the most important tourist attractions in the country. The artist is buried in the town's churchyard, and the interior of the church features his work.

Tel: (46) 23 600 53. www.clg.se. Open: May–Sept daily 10am–5pm; Oct–Apr by appointment. Admission charge.

The castle at Örebro

Nobel Prize

Every year on 10 December the Nobel Prizes for literature, physics, chemistry, medicine and peace are presented to the year's finest achievers, as they have been since 1901. A sixth prize, for work in economics, has been awarded since 1968.

The awards are presented in honour of Alfred Nobel (1833–96), an inventor, chemist and all-round aesthete, who hailed from Stockholm (*see p23*). From an early age Nobel developed a fascination with explosives, and by 1850 he was a gifted chemist, having studied the subject for a year in Paris, and later in the United States. Until that time the most common form of explosive was gunpowder, but in 1862 Nobel built a small factory and began experimenting with nitroglycerin, going on to develop a more powerful incendiary device, as well as a

Nobelmuseet – Alfred Nobel's summer house

detonator to control the chemical's volatility. By 1867 he had learned to combine nitroglycerin with a porous earth compound. This he called dynamite, and patented it internationally. Dynamite was to become a vital driver of the industrial age, enabling constructors to, among other things, blast tunnels through mountains, leading to the creation of roads and railways.

Over the years Nobel continued to modify and improve his invention as well as becoming active in the production of weaponry. Nevertheless he was known as a pacifist and genuinely believed that the creation of more powerful explosives would bring any ensuing wars to a quicker end. This attitude became apparent to the world after his death, when his will revealed that he had left his large fortune to the establishment of a philanthropic award that would honour achievements in artistic, scientific and humanitarian arenas. The reason for his decision is not known, although some believe that, towards the end of his life, Nobel realised that his inventions had brought about much death and carnage, as well as positive

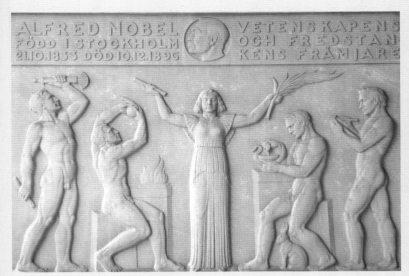

Carved panel on the Alfred Nobel museum in Stockholm

achievements, and he wanted to repent posthumously.

Today the awards are the most prestigious in the world. All of them are awarded in Stockholm, apart from the peace prize, which is awarded in Oslo at Nobel's behest. The annual recipients are selected by an international committee of more than 6,000 people from various learned institutions who present their nominees to the Nobel Foundation in January each year. Much research then ensues regarding the value of the nominees until the winners are announced in November. Apart from the peace prize, the awards are only given to individual achievers, who each receive a gold medal, a diploma and an undisclosed, although substantial, sum of money. Occasionally, however, the prizes are withheld, if there are no significant nominees that year (this is particularly relevant to the peace prize, especially in times of international turmoil).

Among those who have won the Nobel Prize for literature are George Bernard Shaw (1925), T S Eliot (1948), Saul Bellow (1975) and Harold Pinter (2005). Recipients of the peace prize include Theodore Roosevelt (1906), Martin Luther King Jr (1964), Mother Teresa (1979), the Dalai Lama (1989) and, jointly, in 1993, Nelson Mandela and F W de Klerk for their work leading to the abandonment of the South African apartheid regime.

Norrland

One of Sweden's largest areas, but also its least inhabited, the north ranges from beautiful coastland and offshore islands to snow-covered forests and wild national parks. Traditionally it has been an important mining area, but it is also noted for its distinctive Sami culture. Visitors are drawn to the region, much of which lies within the Arctic Circle, to experience two seasonal phenomena: the midnight sun in summer and the northern lights in winter.

SOUTHERN NORRLAND
Älvdalen

Älvdalen's main claim to fame is the production of musical instruments, namely guitars and accordions produced by Albin Hagström, that are now honoured in the **Hagström Museum**. The strong-necked plastic electric guitars in particular were very popular in the 1950s and 1960s, and were even played by legends such as Jimi Hendrix and Elvis Presley. Also on display at the museum are items made out of porphyry, the locally sourced crystal-studded rock.
*Dalagatan 81. Tel: (46) 025 141 035.
Open: mid-Jun–mid-Aug daily
11am–5pm; mid-Aug–mid-Jun Tue–Fri
10am–noon & 1–3pm.
Admission charge.*

Hiking along Norrland's mountains

Åre

Sweden's best-known ski resort owes its success to the high altitude of the Åreskutan mountain, which ensures snow even in June. The resort has been popular since the 19th century, and in addition to excellent downhill skiing there are opportunities for para-skiing and snowmobile trips.

Fulufjället National Park

This forested national park is best known for Sweden's tallest waterfall, Njupeskär, a cascading drop of 97m (318ft). Also within the park is the Altarringen, an ancient religious site that is sacred to the Swedish. Services are still held here regularly. Fishing, hiking, horse riding and canoeing are popular activities in summer, while winter provides opportunities for skiing, dog-sledging and ice fishing. Birdwatchers are also in their element here, with large populations of bluethroats, woodpeckers, cuckoos and owls.

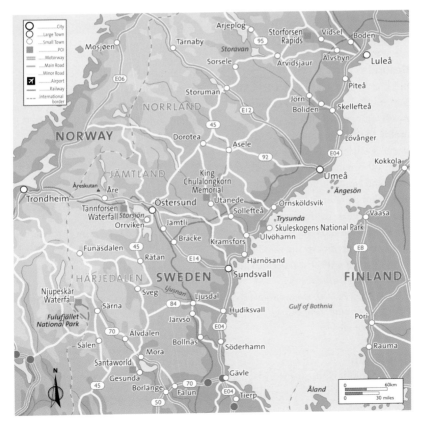

A view of Ljusnan River from Ljusdal

Gesunda

Billed as Santa Claus's 'official' home, Santaworld in the town of Gesunda is awash with excited children all year round. In the log-cabin workshop there is a post office where Santa himself stamps the mail, and a set of mechanical elves who work through the night to make all the presents. In Santa's home there is his chair by the fireplace, a Christmas tree and wrapped presents. Trolls and elves lurk in the woods. In winter there are theatrical performances. *Santaworld, Gesundaberget.*
Tel: (46) 250 287 70. www.santaworld.se.
Open: year round, times vary.
Admission charge.

Härjedalen

This mountain landscape is a magnet for ski enthusiasts, with the main resort towns being located in Funäsdalen, Sveg and Vemdalsfjällen. As well as downhill and cross-country skiing, there is ice fishing and wildlife spotting, and, in summer, mountain biking, hiking and riding on Icelandic horses.

BANDY

Bandy is generally considered to be Sweden's national sport and is similar to ice hockey. During the 90-minute game, played at breakneck speed, 12 players on each team attempt to score goals by putting an orange ball with sticks across an ice rink 110m (361ft) in length. The game took off in Sweden at the turn of the 20th century and rapidly spread throughout the country and the rest of the world. The speed and excitement of the game is reflected in the spirit of the spectators who cheer and beat drums vociferously in support of their teams. Every October the Bandy World Cup is held in Ljusdal, with competitors coming from all over Scandinavia, Russia, Canada and the USA to vie for the ultimate prize.

Härjedalens Fjällmuseum

In the late 19th century a local collector, Erik Fundin, began gathering items of local importance that today form the core of this impressive museum. Exhibits relate mainly to the Sami people, and the lives of local farmers and miners, but there is also a sculpture collection and plenty of activities for children, including a secret tunnel through the surrounding woodlands.
Funäsdalen. Tel: (46) 684 155 80.
Open: Mon–Fri 9am–5pm, Sat & Sun noon–4pm. Admission charge.

Härnösand

This charming coastal town has been a thriving trading post since the 16th century, and was an important defence area during the threat of Russian invasion in the 18th century. Today it is a popular summer resort with its beaches and yacht harbour.

Länsmuseet Västernorrland

The town's open-air museum preserves 18th-century buildings as well as exhibits detailing the region's agricultural heritage and timber industry, and a large collection of firearms.
Murberget, Härnösand.
Tel: (46) 0611 886 00.
Open: Tue–Sun 11am–5pm.
Admission charge (free on Fri).

Ljusdal

Set on the Ljusnan River, this pretty town has been a centre of activity since the 12th century. Part of the town's church still dates from the Middle Ages, although the bell tower with its distinctive dome was constructed in the 1750s. Just south of the town is Järvsö, a nature park with a boardwalk where you can watch indigenous creatures such as brown bears and wolves in their natural habitat. White-water rafting and longboat rowing are also available nearby.

Östersund

Östersund is best known for the Storsjön monster, which is thought to survive in the lake surrounding the town (*see pp148–9*). The town is set in a region known as Jämtland, which was autonomous until a Norwegian takeover in the 12th century, and the people still set themselves apart from mainstream Swedish culture with pride. One of the highlights of the year here is the winter market in early March, where the proud traditions of the locals come to the fore.

A game of bandy

Jämtli

The town's main museum is a wonderfully evocative insight into life in the region over the centuries, featuring home interiors, farmsteads and various other interactive exhibits that genuinely give a sense of living and breathing history. Even the on-site restaurant re-creates a similar establishment from the 1940s. The most famous exhibit is the 12th-century Överhogdal Tapestry depicting hunters, animals and other aspects of Viking life – thought to be the oldest surviving tapestry in Europe. In summer there is an open-air area with animals native to the region, and a great deal of activities aimed at children.

Museiplan. Tel: (46) 063 15 01 00. www.jamtli.com. Open: mid-Jun–Aug 11am–5pm daily; Sept–mid-Jun Tue–Sun 11am–5pm. Admission charge.

Moose Garden

Children will particularly enjoy Östersund's moose garden, where you can get up close and personal with these beautiful animals, help with the feeding, as well as learn about the production of 'moose paper', made from the animals' droppings, which contains cellulose to help with the process.

Orrviken 145. Tel: (46) 063 404 80. www.moosegarden.com. Open: for tours daily 11am, 1pm & 3pm. Admission charge.

Sälen

Traditionally this was the starting point for the Vasaloppet ski race (it now starts from a larger area in Berga), and it still remains a popular centre for winter sports, with ski pistes to suit all levels of ability. The town's heritage centre, Olnispagården, re-creates a farmstead of the 18th and 19th centuries, complete with cowsheds, workers' cottages and a blacksmith's.

Olnispagården open: mid-May–mid-Jun & mid-Aug–mid-Sept daily 10am–3pm; mid-Jun–mid-Aug 10am–6pm. Admission charge.

Skuleskogens National Park

Mountain and forest trails are protected within the 30sq km (11½sq miles) making up this national park. It forms part of an area known as the High Coast, which was designated a UNESCO World Natural Heritage Site in 2000.

Söderhamn

The most recognisable feature of this town is the Oscarsborg, a tall lookout tower looming over the surrounding area. The town was constantly under threat from Russian invasion in the 18th century and for this reason the area became a centre for ammunitions production, all of which is documented in the town museum.

Sundsvall

In the late 19th century Sundsvall was devastated by a town fire, and had to be completely rebuilt. The town today is a beautifully preserved area of ornate 1890s stone architecture, including the Town Hall (*Stadhuset*) and the Hirschska Huset, which is decorated with the town's symbol of a dragon, intended to protect it from more fires. The most famous building in town, however, is the luxurious Knaust Hotel, built in 1891, with its wonderful sweeping staircase. Near the harbour, on Sjögatan, four former warehouses have also been preserved and masterfully converted into the town's cultural centre. Sundsvall truly bursts into life each July when one of the country's largest street festivals, the Gatufesten, takes place here, featuring a range of activities and concerts by international artists (*see p26*).

Tännforsen Waterfall

The most powerful waterfall in the country gushes at breakneck speed, churning 700m³ (24,720cu ft) of water down a 38m (125ft) drop. No one can fail to be inspired by the sheer force and magnitude of nature in such a setting.

Trysunda

Lying just off the mainland, this picturesque island consists of a traditional fishing village and is lined with red-painted wooden houses and an attractive 17th-century church. The town is best known as a tranquil summer spot for swimming and sailing, but if you're interested in the history of the place visit the Fishing Museum where exhibits explain fishing techniques practised over the centuries.

Inside the lookout tower of Söderhamn

Ulvöhamn

Surströmming is a speciality of this town and this region, but the fermented herring concoction is definitely an acquired taste. It is traditionally eaten outdoors in autumn with onions and potatoes, and washed down with milk, schnapps, *aquavit* or beer. The town's most famous building is its 17th-century chapel, with a fresco dating from 1718.

Utanede

One of the most unusual sights on the Swedish landscape has to be the King Chulalongkorn Memorial, a Thai pavilion that was built to commemorate the centenary of the King of Siam's visit to the area in 1897. The pavilion, the largest of its kind outside Thailand, was designed in its native country, and the parts then dispatched to Sweden for assembly in

The lookout tower of Söderhamn

1997. It is a particularly bizarre sight in winter, when the exotic edifice is covered with glistening white snow.
Tel: (46) 696 321 06.
Open: mid-May–mid-Sept daily 10am–5pm. Free admission.

NORTHERN NORRLAND
Boden

The most famous feature of Boden, which has a long military history, is the Rödbergsfortet bunker, which is hewn into the rock. It is now open to the public, despite having been a guarded secret for many years.

Garnmuseet (Garrison Museum)

For a fuller explanation of Boden's military history, there's no better place than the Garrison Museum. Among the exhibits are military uniforms,

a re-creation of a soldier's living quarters and various pieces of artillery and other soldiering equipment.
Sveavägen 10. Tel: (46) 921 683 99.
Open: mid-Jun–mid-Aug daily 10am–4pm. Admission charge (free on Fri).

Western Farm

This slightly incongruous theme park re-creates the American Wild West, complete with saloons, staged shoot-outs, old-fashioned stores and a resident sheriff. Visitors can ride like cowboys, hunt out villains and basically let their John Wayne imaginations run wild.
Buddbyvägen 6.
Tel: (46) 921 151 00.
www.western-farm.com. Open: July Wed 4–9pm. Admission charge.

Thai pavilion, Utanede

Boliden

The two largest gold mines in Europe are located here, and the history of the mining industry, which lasted from 1924 to 1967, can be uncovered at the gold-mine museum, the Bergrum Boliden, which also explores the geological history of gold in this part of the world. Also of note here is the world's longest cable-car line, built to transport gold ore.

Lövånger

Lövånger was set up in medieval times as a central meeting point for Christians from rural villages, who came here to worship during festivals. Because they all lived at a considerable distance from the nearest church, which was erected here in the 16th century, they stayed over in the wooden cabins that line the streets, some of which are now used as tourist accommodation. The history of Lövånger, and the many other church villages like it in the region, can be discovered at the Sockenmuseet, which is next to the church.

Luleå

The capital of northern Sweden has been a thriving area since the Middle Ages, and its Old Town area (Gammelstad) preserves a collection of traditional architecture in what has now been designated a UNESCO World Heritage Site. The most distinctive feature is the medieval church, surrounding which is a collection of more than 400 wooden cabins built as accommodation for worshippers from outlying regions. The church's 16th-century altar was designed in Belgium.

Teknikens Hus (House of Technology)

For those more interested in the future than the past, a visit to this science centre, 5km (3 miles) outside Luleå, is a must. Make your own paper, or try your hand at launching a rocket. There's a planetarium as well.
Tel: (46) 920 49 22 01.
www.teknikenshus.se.
Open: Tue–Fri 10am–4pm, Sat & Sun 11am–4pm. Admission charge.

Piteå

In the summer months, when the sun barely sets, the population of Piteå more than doubles, as visitors flock to its many beaches, inlets and islands. But in addition to all the outdoor activities, the town is proud of its culture and draws artists, craftsmen and musicians. The town's museum on the main square (Storgatan) details the history of the district. Also in town is an impressive medieval church, the Öjeby Kyrka.

Storforsen Rapids

With drops of over 82m (269ft) and covering an area of 5km (3 miles), these are among the most impressive rapids in the country. Part of the rapids, known as Dead Falls, is inadvertently man-made. Attempts in 1796 to block off the water to facilitate transportation of timber logs went wrong. A massive flood occurred that drained this part of the rapids, leaving behind mysterious rock cauldrons.

Umeå

With its streets framed by birch trees, most of Umeå's present townscape dates back to the 19th century when the city was rebuilt after a fire, although the town was first established in the 17th century.

Västerbottens Museum

The town's main museum focuses on the history of the area, and includes an open-air area in summer displaying traditional rural homes. In summer there are great opportunities for leisurely canoeing or energy-pumping whitewater rafting in the surrounding region.
Gammlia. Tel: (46) 090 17 18 00.
Open: July Mon–Sat 8am–4pm;
Sept–Jun Tue–Thur 10am–4pm.
Free admission.

LAPLAND
Arjeplog

The heartbeat of this town is the silver-mining industry, so it is an apt location for a museum dedicated to the precious metal. On display are items of silver Sami jewellery and crockery as well as exhibits detailing the lives of the local people. The museum was set up using the collections of a local doctor who was charmed by the area, and, as part of the exhibits, his house has been preserved as it was during the 1920s.
Silvermuseet: Torget.
Tel: (46) 961 61290.
www.silvermuseet.arjeplog.se. Open:
Jun–mid-Aug daily 9am–6pm; mid-Aug–May Mon–Fri 10am–4pm, Sat 10am–2pm. Admission charge.

Norrland

A view of the mountains in Kiruna, Lapland

Arvidsjaur

This small lakeside town has been a centre of Sami trade since ancient times, and the Sami village area (Lappstaden) makes for a fascinating insight into the culture and traditions of this ethnic group. The excellently preserved Sami church village was the centre of converted Sami Christians from around the region, who came here to worship and stayed in the basic wooden huts constructed for this purpose.

Jokkmokk

Jokkmokk is one of Sweden's most renowned and popular Sami towns and one of the best places to hunt for authentic Sami handicrafts. The most famous event here occurs every February, as it has for the last 400 years: the Saturday Sami winter market to which people flock from all around. Despite the dark days when the sun barely rises, there is a carnival-like atmosphere with brightly coloured

Lapland

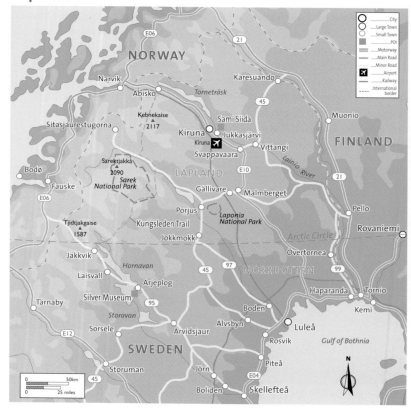

stalls as well as reindeer races and many other festivities. Also of note is the Lapp Kyrka, in which local Sami residents would bury their dead in winter in wall vaults until the summer thaw allowed them to dig burial sites in the ground outside.

Ájtte

As the heartland for the region's Sami community, Jokkmokk is also a fitting setting for a Sami museum that details the history of their culture and their daily lives.
Kyrkogatan 3. Tel: (46) 0971 170 70.
Open: Jun–Aug daily 9am–6pm;
Sept–May Mon–Fri 9am–6pm.
Admission charge.

Kiruna

The capital of the Lapland region of Sweden is also the centre of one of the world's largest municipalities – only Australia can boast a larger one in Brisbane. Despite its size, however, it is one of the most sparsely populated areas of the country. Much of its history, like the rest of the north, was centred on mining, particularly iron ore. Its other claim to fame is as home to the country's tallest mountain, Kebnekaise, at 2,117m (6,946ft). If visiting the region between December and April, don't miss the opportunity of staying at the unique Icehotel (*see p178*).

Dog sledging

One of the most popular activities in the Kiruna region is dog sledging.

Various companies offer day tours or longer, and supply all necessary equipment. Training is given in how to ride the sledge as well as how to handle the excitable, athletic husky dogs, as you glide speedily through the forests and the tundra.
Tel: (46) 980 50030.
www.kirunanature.com

InfoMine

Kiruna is home to the largest underground iron ore mine in the world and the source of much of the region's wealth in days gone by and the present day. Guided tours allow visitors to descend 540m (1,772ft) into the mine to understand current mining techniques, while the mining museum explores the history of the industry, the discovery and development of this

MIDNIGHT SUN AND THE NORTHERN LIGHTS

For those wishing to see these summer and winter phenomena, Kiruna is an ideal base. In summer the sun never sets beneath the horizon between June and mid-July and there is daylight for about 20 hours a day, a phenomenon known as the midnight sun, or polar day. In contrast, in winter, there are some 20 days between mid-December and mid-January when the sun never rises, known as the polar night. During the winter the northern lights (*aurora borealis*) can occur, when energy particles interact with the magnetic atmosphere and create a strange vision of 'dancing' yellow and green lights in the night sky. For those visiting northern Sweden in winter this is one of the most spectacular sights of the region.

Dog sledging is an exhilarating way to view the ice-covered landscape

mine, and the lives of the miners.
Lars Jansongatan 17. Tel: (46) 980 18286. Open: Aug daily 9am–noon & 2–5pm; Sept–Dec 9am–noon & 1–4pm. Admission charge.

Kiruna Church

The most striking building in Kiruna is its church, built in 1912 in the shape of a Sami tent (*goahti*). The church has been voted the most beautiful building in Sweden, and its altar was painted by Prince Eugen, a member of the royal family and a great landscape artist.
Kyrkogatan 8. Tel: (46) 980 67800.

Sami Siida

Just outside the main town of Kiruna, this Sami cultural centre allows visitors to immerse themselves in the traditional Sami way of life, including reindeer sledge rides, authentic Sami cuisine such as reindeer stew eaten in a Sami tent, and hunting trips. There are also two museums displaying various aspects of Sami culture, including costumes, musical instruments and

tools, while the shop is an excellent place to buy souvenir jewellery or knives, with the added bonus of knowing that they have been authentically produced.
Marknadsvägen 11, Jukkasjärvi. Tel: (46) 980 21329. www.nutti.se. Museum open: mid-Dec–mid-Apr daily 10am–6pm. Admission charge.

Lainio River

Dating from the 17th century, Lainio has always been a traditional meeting point between the northern Swedish and Sami cultures, but today, set in a stunning landscape, it is best known by avid anglers. Salmon, trout and grayling are the prime catches, but there are also abundant supplies of pike and char. In addition to fishing, there are

REINDEER

Reindeer (*Rangifer tarandus*), also known as caribou in America, are ideally suited to their Arctic environment, possessing hooves that can withstand extreme cold on the ice, and a double-layered coat that preserves heat. They are also capable of covering vast distances, some estimates being given at 5,000km (3,107 miles) per year, as well as being skilled swimmers, both of which are necessary for the beasts to find grazing land throughout the year. Their relationship with the Sami community can be seen as symbiotic; the Sami provide the reindeer with food, while the animals' hide provides warm clothing and blankets, they facilitate transportation and their milk and meat is the staple Sami diet. By law, in Sweden, only the Sami people are allowed to engage in reindeer herding and they can do so on both public and private land.

opportunities for canoeing and hunting, and even gold panning in summer.

Laponia National Park

In 1996 UNESCO granted World Heritage status to the mountainous region of Lapland known as Laponia. For centuries the area has been home to nomadic Sami reindeer herders, but it is its geological development and environmental importance as a habitat for indigenous flora and fauna that earned it its protected status. Within the more than 9,000sq km (3,475sq miles) there are four national parks, with ample hiking possibilities.

Sarek National Park

For experienced and confident hikers, there can be nothing more magical than trekking the stunning wilderness of this park filled with more than 100 glaciers, numerous mountains and inhabited by bears and lynx. The park is incorporated within the Kungsleden (King's) Trail, established in the 1900s for avid walkers, but conditions and weather are tough and trails are unmarked, so it is certainly not for the novice or the under-equipped. Most of the facilities, such as huts and bridges, have been put in place primarily for use by Sami reindeer herders, so their condition cannot be guaranteed.

A reindeer sledge and riders

Myths and legends

Before Christianity came to Sweden a large majority of the population believed in pagan myths that helped them make sense of their landscape, climate and disasters, such as crop failures, illnesses and shipwrecks. Despite modern religion, science and technology there's still a palpable sense of this heritage today, in the many myths and legends that continue to form part of the Swedish mindset.

In Norse mythology, which also embraces Norway, Denmark and Iceland, Thor, the god of thunder, was seen as the most powerful being, who could destroy anything in his path if riled by wielding his mighty hammer and delivering fatal bolts of lightning. The most revered god, however, was the one-eyed Odin, the father of all living things and a figure of wisdom. He was the only god to be worshipped in the manner that we now associate with modern religion. The Vikings, in particular, looked to Odin to bless them before embarking on their voyages. Odin presided over Valhalla (heaven), where the female Valkyries were responsible for the fate of Viking warriors.

Besides the gods, there were other mythical creatures that were thought to govern the landscape. Whereas Norway retains a faith in trolls, Sweden maintains a strong conviction in dwarves (*huldra*) and elves (*älvor*). They are said to inhabit the country's hills and forests. While generally light-hearted and harmless, they are believed to turn nasty if annoyed and are capable of inflicting pain and disease.

However, the most famous Swedish myth is from more recent times, and is very real for some believers even today. It is that of the *Storsjöodjuret*, a monster thought to inhabit the depths of Lake Storsjön in the

Sculpture of a mythical beast

The monster of Lake Storsjön

Jämtland region in north Sweden (*see p137*). Similar to Scotland's Loch Ness monster, lore has variously described the 'beast' as a relic of the dinosaur era, a deformed and therefore oversized fish or seal, or simply as an accumulation of gas bubbling beneath the water's surface. Legend also has it that the monster was created in the 17th century by two evil witches, who conjured it from a special brew. By the 19th century fascination had built to such a level that even the king commissioned an operation to capture the beast with a harpoon, but this came to nothing.

According to the hundreds of 'witnesses' over the centuries, the monster takes the form of a large, humped creature, with a long neck and a horse-like head. It was apparently caught on film as recently as 1996, and, in 1998, another expedition set out to investigate, but nothing conclusive was found. Nevertheless the government and the county take the monster very seriously, not least as a tourist attraction, and have made the lake a protected area and set up official observation sites, from where visitors are told they are most likely to get a sighting.

The Samis

It is estimated that there are around 17,000 Samis living in Sweden, belonging to an ethnic race whose members are spread across the Lapland region of northern Norway, Finland and Russia. In Sweden they make their home in the northern region of Kiruna and the surrounding area, making up ten per cent of the population in that vicinity (*see pp145–6*).

It is thought that the Samis arrived in the region around 1,000 years ago; they are known to have traded with the Vikings and the Hanseatic League.

Traditional Sami clothing

Over the centuries attempts were made to assimilate them into the overall population of the countries within which they lived, but in 1956 the Nordic Sami Council was set up to protect their individual status. It brought them official recognition as a separate indigenous group. Today the Sami have their own semi-autonomous parliament, the *Sametinget*, whose job it is to promote and preserve their culture and language, both in society and in local schools. They also advise the Swedish parliament on Sami issues. All Samis and their descendants are allowed to vote in the Sametinget.

The Sami language bears no resemblance to Swedish; it is instead a Finno-Ugric tongue, with links to both Finnish and Hungarian. Within this there are also several dialects. All Sami children, however, are required to learn Swedish as well as their mother tongue, and the Sami language is not used in any official context, not even in the Sami parliament. In the Sami region there are separate Sami schools where lessons are taught bilingually.

The Samis who continue to live a traditional lifestyle largely earn their livelihood through reindeer herding,

An audience at the Ice Globe Theatre

using the now semi-domesticated animals for their own transportation, but also for trading in reindeer skin and meat. The fact that the Sami language has around 400 different words for reindeer clearly illustrates the importance of this beast to the community. Other income comes from fishing and the production of the distinctive red, white and blue costumes and handicrafts, which are picked up by tourists. However, earning enough via traditional means is becoming increasingly hard and many younger Samis have begun to migrate to and enrol in more commercial professions in the big cities.

The Samis follow an animistic religion, meaning that they assign souls to all manner of things including the landscape, animals and geological aspects. In terms of the arts, the Sami tradition of *yoik* (chanting) as a means of telling stories and sagas is seeing something of a revival these days, largely because of tourism. In fact, tourism is becoming one of the most important sources of income, with enterprises such as the Ice Hotel (*see p178*) and its adjacent Ice Globe Theatre (*see p165*), a Sami version of Shakespeare's Globe in London, drawing visitors in droves.

Getting away from it all

Few countries offer better opportunities for isolation and tranquillity than Sweden, with its vast landscape and sparse population. Even in the cities there is an abundance of parkland where you can always find a quiet spot to soak up your surroundings. In the south the many islands dotted around the coast have tiny populations and long beaches, while the northern forests define the term 'wilderness'.

Urban nature

Few capital cities offer as much nature as Stockholm. On the island of Djurgården (*see pp37–41*) there's a national city park, known as the Ecopark, with opportunities for cycling, horse riding and sailing in summer and ice-skating in winter. Then, of course, there are the islands, and there can't be anything more relaxing than taking one of the many ferries that operate from the harbour and gliding slowly across the water, taking in the city's skyline and the beautiful wooded vistas.

Lakes and canals

The west of Sweden is the prime area for lakeland adventures, with the region around the Dalsand Canal (*see p94*) offering a range of activities, from sailing and canoeing, to fishing, hiking and cycling. Avid anglers should also head for Lake Vänern (*see p98 & p101*) or Lake Hallsjön where the waters are rich in salmon, trout, pike and perch.

Spas

Spas are not a big thing in Sweden – after all, with so much natural landscape, why restrict yourself to a dedicated resort? However, it is home to the oldest spa in Scandinavia, **Medevi Brunn**. The resort opened in the 17th century when the spring waters here were found to have healing properties by a local doctor. For six weeks each summer visitors have the opportunity to not only take the waters, but also explore the historic buildings, enjoy nightly concerts and take part in activities such as miniature golf.
Road No 50, north of Motala.
Tel: (46) 141 911 00.
Open mid-Jun–mid-Aug.

Timber rafting

The Klarälven River in western Svealand near Hagefors has been a major log-driving route since the 18th century, and today it is renowned for its peaceful timber-rafting activities for tourists. Various companies along the river supply the logs and rope, and instructions on how to build a raft, then leave you to your own devices, gliding peacefully along the calm waters through the forested landscape. Although in reality you're never far from the next village and any necessary supplies or aid, there's a real sense of adventure to the trip. If you're lucky you'll also see native beavers in the water and along the riverbanks. Trips last between one and seven days, with a minimum of

two people and a maximum of six per raft.
www.videmark.se

Island hopping

The most popular area for island hopping in Sweden is around Stockholm, but for a more singular experience head north to the area known as the High Coast on the Gulf of Bothnia. Here, islands such as Ulvöhamn and Trysunda (*see pp139–40*) offer traditional fishing villages, quiet

A traditional Swedish summer house

Dog sledging across northern Sweden's tundra landscape

inlets and coves ideal for swimming, as well as historic churches and fishermen's huts. Ferries ply the waters daily in summer and there's overnight accommodation on the islands.

On the west coast the many closely linked islands north and south of Gothenburg offer ideal kayaking adventures covering short distances, and a right-of-access law means that camping and cooking freshly caught fish over a campfire are possible at most places. *For more information visit www.kanotguiden.com*

True wilderness

Sarek National Park (*see p147*) is not for the inexperienced, but for those with the know-how to survive in the wild there can be no greater sense of getting away from it all. More than 5,000sq km (1,931sq miles) of trackless landscape on the northern border with Norway offer dramatic gorges and glaciers, primeval forests and ravines. Bears and wolverines, as well as a large population of elk, inhabit this mountainous and untamed park.

Dog and reindeer sledging

In Sweden's Lapland region various companies offer sledging trips pulled by either husky dogs or reindeer, which is a spectacular and exhilarating way to take in the sparse, icy landscape. Overnight accommodation can be arranged in log cabins or Sami tents, and traditional Sami food, such as reindeer stew, is cooked over an open fire.
www.laplandwildernesstours.com

Wildlife watching

Many different areas of Sweden offer opportunities for spotting indigenous wildlife and getting to grips with nature. In the north overnight moose safaris attempt to spot elk in their natural habitat of snow-covered forests at dusk and dawn, while in Dalarna in western Svealand, organised guided trips track wolves around the Lake Sijan area. Birdwatchers should head for the Lilla Karlsö area (*see p107*), a nature reserve that is home to peregrine falcons and guillemots, or the southern part of the island of Öland, where migratory birds such as redshanks and grebes make their temporary base.

Ljunga river landscape

Shopping

One of the joys of shopping in Sweden is finding products where great attention has been paid to design (see pp90–91). Stockholm, in particular, is one of the most stylish shopping cities in Europe.

Swedish specialities that make ideal souvenirs or gifts include the traditional painted Dala wooden horses (*see p129*), glass and crystal pieces (*see pp88–9*), food delicacies such as herring rollmops and cloudberry jam, and, in the north, Sami handicrafts. Most tourist areas are also awash with Viking paraphernalia, which is particularly popular with children. Swedish schnapps is also a popular gift; but note that alcohol in Sweden can only be purchased at shops known as *Systembolaget* and the minimum age for buying alcohol is 20.

Markets can be found in most towns particularly during summer weekends, but one of the most famous takes place in February in the town of Jokkmokk (*see pp144–5*), and is the best place for Sami items.

STOCKHOLM

While Stockholm city centre is the main shopping area, there are also plenty of smaller and more individual shops on the islands of Gamla Stan and Södermalm. The main department store is **Nordiska Kompaniet**, known as NK (*see pp52–3*), which houses all the international designer names. There are also malls such as **Gallerien** (*Hamngatan 37*) and **Sturegallerien** (*Grev Turegatan 9*) that house numerous outlets, such as Benetton, French Connection and The Body Shop. For standard souvenirs, head for Västerlånggatan in Gamla Stan (*see p44*). For designer names such as Gucci and Armani the Östermalm district is the place to go.

Björn Borg Store

The former tennis ace Björn Borg now runs a chain of stores selling sportswear and accessories.
Sergelgatan 12. Tel: (46) 821 70 40.

Blås & Knåda

This is the place to come for the largest selection of traditional Swedish glassware and ceramics.

Hornsgatan 26. Tel: (46) 864 277 67.
www.blasknada.com

Duka

An Old Town souvenir shop that is a
cut above the rest, with beautiful and
innovative crystal glass items, textiles,
toys and various representations of
Sweden's myths and legends.
Järntorget 78. Tel: (46) 822 88 07.
www.duka.se

Nordiska Galleriet

In business since 1913, this is one of the
best-known places in the city for stylish
and elegant modern furniture and
household accessories.
Nybrogatan 11. Tel: (46) 844 283 60.
www.nordiskagalleriet.se

Östermalms Market Hall

Stockholm's most famous food market
offers a mouth-watering array of
Swedish delicacies, such as fresh crab,
herring, cloudberries and reindeer

meat. There is also a range of cafés and
restaurants within the complex. Not
to be missed for its bustling atmosphere
and wonderful aromas. Other food
markets are Söderhallarna and
Hötorgshallen.
Slakthusplan 3. Tel: (46) 508 466 66.

Retro Home

Stockholm has developed a fine
reputation for antiques in recent years,
and this is an ideal stop if you're in
search of classic Scandinavian
furniture, glassware or ceramics
from different eras of the
20th century.
Kindstugatan 7. Tel: (46) 831 21 30.

10-Gruppen

On the island of Södermalm, which has
a reputation as the trendiest area in the
city, this offbeat shop sells quirky items
such as plastic handbags and
psychedelic ironing-board covers.
Götgatan 25. Tel: (46) 864 325 04.

Stockholm's Nordiska Kompaniet shows elegant design at every corner

Stock up at a deli for a picnic

GOTHENBURG

Like Stockholm, Gothenburg has a range of department stores and malls, such as Nordstan on Brunnsparken. There are also a number of markets. The most famous shopping area is Avenyn (*see p56*), with a wide range of fashion stores, interior design emporia and bookshops, to name just a few.

Arkivet

Here you'll find photo albums, notebooks, ink stamps, greetings cards, artists' materials and paper in a rainbow of colours. A haven for those with artistic leanings.
Arkivgatan 4.

Bohusslöjd

Woodwork, textiles, leather and ceramics all produced in traditional styles can be found here. A one-stop shop for authentic souvenirs.
Teatergatan 19. Tel: (46) 311 600 72.

Elvis Unlimited

Anyone with a remote interest in the 'King' should head to this specialist shop, which is said to be the greatest gathering of Elvis Presley memorabilia outside Memphis. Records, clothing, posters and even autographs are on sale here.
Teatergatan 15. Tel: (46) 311 182 828.
www.elvisunlimited.se

F

If you're into 1960s kitsch, this is the place for you. Bakelite telephones, plastic furniture, vinyl records and all manner of Pop Art items are displayed in all their colourful glory.
Andra Långgatan 18.

Haga Interiör

One of the best interior design boutiques in the trendy old district of Haga, incorporating the best of Swedish style.
Haga Nygata 33A. Tel: (46) 311 338 21.

Saluhallen

Gothenburg's food market is an aromatic delight of fresh bread, roasted coffee, cheeses and herbs. The market has been in operation since the 19th century. There are also restaurants and cafés where you can sample some of the produce on sale.

Kungstorget. Tel: (46) 311 775 30.

MALMÖ

The main shopping area of the city is pedestrianised and runs from the main square – Gustav Adolfs Torg – along Södergatan. All the usual chains and department stores can be found here, as well as the Galleri Storgatan that is unique to Malmö. On the last Saturday of every month, known as 'long Saturday', department stores stay open until 5pm (they close at 3pm on other Saturdays) and usually have special offers and discounts, so this is a good day to shop if you're in the city at that time. Möllevångstorget is the place to go for various food emporia selling international ingredients.

Designtorget

An eclectic array of Swedish arts and crafts, including wooden toys, stationery, glassware, ceramics, linen and children's clothes.

Södra Vallgatan 3. Tel: (40) 307 082. www.designtorget.se

Form/Design Center

As well as a shop selling all manner of design classics in glass, ceramics and textiles, furniture and books on Swedish design, this is an exhibition space, and lectures on design are occasionally held in the bright and airy café.

Hedmanska Gården, Lilla Torg. Tel: (40) 664 5150. www.formdesigncenter.com

Les Trois Roses

Anyone with a sweet tooth will be at home with this chocolatier.

Gustav Adolfs Torg 43. Tel: (40) 122 212.

Möllans Ost

The finest gourmet shop in town, selling cheeses, truffles, marmalade and jams and Italian hams. If you can manage to carry them, the hampers are irresistible buys.

Bergsgatan 32c. Tel: (40) 193 545. www.mollansost.com

Norrgavel

If you're in the mood for traditional Swedish style, in the vogue of Carl Larsson (*see p90 & p131*), this is the place for you. The textiles, furniture and ornaments are all inspired by Swedish folk and rural traditions.

Engelbrektsgatan 20. Tel: (40) 122 246. www.norrgavel.se

Malls offer plentiful shopping

Entertainment

Sweden has a long tradition of theatre and music and in all its cities you'll find plenty to entertain, from classical and contemporary productions to outdoor festivals in summer, making fine use of the extra hours of daylight. Nightlife in Stockholm and Gothenburg is thumping all year round, and the nation's love of jazz means that some of the most exciting clubs in Europe can be found here.

TOURIST INFORMATION AND TICKETS

Tourist information offices in all important towns and cities will have up-to-date information about what is on during your stay and can offer advice about how to book tickets and how to get to the venue. For those interested in the cultural life of a place, this should be the first port of call. The official tourist website (*www.visit-sweden.com*) will also have information on events coming up, and if you want to book tickets in advance log on to the national booking outfit **Bilkett Direkt** (*www.ticnet.se – in Swedish only*).

STOCKHOLM
Cinema

All foreign films are subtitled in Swedish, so any British or American imports are screened in their original language and are, therefore, accessible to English-speaking tourists. Cinemas can be found all over the city centre and films reach Sweden at approximately the same time as the rest of northern Europe. The **Cosmonova** complex has an IMAX theatre, as well as a restaurant and bar. *Frescativägen 40. Tel: (08) 519 540 40.*

Clubs and bars
Café Opera

The city's best-known bar is housed in the Opera House, with all its beautiful *belle époque* décor incorporated within the context of a modern and stylish drinking spot.
Operahuset. Karl XII Torg.
Tel: (08) 67 658 07.
Admission charge.

Eriks Gondolen

At the top of the Katrinahissen, this wine bar not only has a comprehensive list of fine wines and British and Belgian beers, it offers superb views of the Stockholm skyline too.
Stadsgården 6. Tel: (08) 64 170 90.
www.eriks.se

Glenfiddich Warehouse No 68

In the tourist heart of the Old Town, this stylish bar serves 16 types of Swedish beer and 160 types of whisky from all over the world.

Västerlänggatan 68.
Tel: (08) 791 90 90.
Open: Mon–Tue 11.30am–11pm, Wed–Fri 11.30am–midnight, Sat noon–midnight.

La Habana

If you're in the mood for a bit of salsa dancing, rum cocktails and an all-round lively Latin ambience, this is the place to be. Cuban food served.

Sveavägen 108.
Tel: (08) 16 64 65.
Open: Mon–Sat 5pm–1am.

Half Way Inn

This small and intimate Scottish pub has become popular for its selection of malt whiskies and its cosy atmosphere.

Swedenborgsgatan 6.
Tel: (08) 64 194 43.

Jazzclub Fasching

The city's number-one jazz club features a nightly programme of Swedish and international jazz artists.

Kungsgatan 63.
Tel: (08) 534 829 60.

Josefina

In summer months the grassy mounds in front of the Nordiska Museum on Djurgården are abuzz with Stockholm's 'beautiful people'. Enjoy drinks here on wicker sofas and brightly coloured cushions in the sunshine, looking out over the Old Town waterfront. There's also a restaurant.

Galärvarvsvägen 10.
Tel: (08) 664 10 04.

Enjoying a drink at Josefina on Djurgården

Kharma

One of the most stylish bars in town, with comfy sofas, a neon-lit bar and a long list of cocktails. Thursday night is gay night.
Sturegatan 10.
Tel: (08) 662 04 65. Open: Thur–Sat 10pm–3am.

Naglo Vodkabar

Wash down a plate of caviar with one of more than 60 types of vodka.
Regeringsgatan 4.
Tel: (08) 10 27 57.

Soldaten Svejk

In this family-run Czech bar ten Czech beers are served on tap, including Gambrinus and Budvar, as well as classic Czech dishes such as gulasch and dumplings.
Östgötagatan 35.
Tel: (08) 641 33 66.
Open: Mon–Thur 5pm–midnight, Fri–Sat 5pm–1am, Sun 5–11pm.

Music

Berwaldhallen

Considered one of the world's most accomplished a cappella choirs, the Swedish Radio Choir is now one of the finest cultural experiences in the country.
Dag Hammarskjölds Väg 3. Tel: (08) 784 18 00.

Folkoperan

Its unusual productions, intimate setting and quality of performance have earned this opera company a well-deserved international reputation.
Hornsgatan 72.
Tel: (08) 616 07 00.

Konserthuset

One of the most impressive features of the Stockholm Concert House, opened in 1926, is its enormous organ, as well as the neoclassical design of the building. Today it is home to the Swedish Royal Philharmonic Orchestra (*see p34*).

Royal Opera House

All the classics of the opera repertoire such as *Tosca* and *The Marriage of Figaro* are staged here as part of an ever-changing annual programme (*see p53*).

Skansen

At certain times of the year, such as Walpurgis Night (*see p26*), Midsummer's Eve and Christmas, folk musicians perform traditional music at this wonderful open-air museum (*see p39*).

Theatre

Göta Lejon

This is the setting for touring Broadway musical productions such as *Grease*, *Jesus Christ Superstar* and *Buddy*.
Götagatan 55.
Tel: (08) 643 67 00.

Kungliga Dramatiska Teatern

The Royal Dramatic Theatre opened in 1908 and is still the premier theatre in the country for both classical and contemporary productions on its total of six stages (*see p35*).

GOTHENBURG

Cinema

Filmstaden Downtown

The largest cinema complex in Gothenburg,

with a total of 16 screens showing all the latest films.
Kungsgatan 35.
Tel: (031) 562 600 00.

Hagabion

The city's arthouse cinema often features specialised programmes as part of a theme, such as Gay Film Week or Women's Cinema. There's also an excellent café here.
Linnégatan 21.
Tel: (031) 42 27 99.

Clubs and bars
Dojan

The oldest and largest music bar in the city, the Dojan has a dance floor on the ground floor and a bar featuring rock music in the basement.
Vallgatan 3.
Tel: (031) 711 2410.
Live music: Thur, Fri & Sat nights.

Harry's

An all-round entertainment venue offering stand-up comedy, a popular, if slightly uncool, disco and a sports bar.
Vasagaten 43.
Tel: (031) 81 2812.

Henriksberg

A combined restaurant, bar and nightclub, the Henriksberg benefits from a roof terrace with wonderful views.
Stigbergsliden 7.
Tel: (031) 24 8200.
www.henriksberg.com

Jazzå Bar

One of the best places to go in Gothenburg if you want to listen to jazz and blues in a comfortable and intimate atmosphere.
Andra Långgatan 4b.

Nefertiti

The best-known jazz club in town, with a programme of international artists.
Hvitfeldtsplatsen 6.
Tel: (031) 711 40 76.

The Royal Dramatic Theatre in Stockholm

Young folk dancers in traditional costume

Ölhallen 7:an
A noisy, dark beer hall with a traditional, laid-back ambience.
Kungstorget 7.
Tel: (031) 13 60 79.

Sticky Fingers
One of the most popular places in town, with a focus on heavy metal and hard rock, although different music is played on each of the three floors. A real heart-pumping experience.
Kaserntorget 7.
Tel: (031) 701 00 17.

Music and theatre
Gothenburg Opera House
This modern opera house, opened in 1994, has quickly become a mainstay of the city's cultural scene. The programme includes contemporary opera, ballet and Broadway musicals (*see p60*).

Konserthuset
Gothenburg's concert hall is home to the city's Symphony Orchestra, which performs more than 100 concerts here every year, apart from international tours. A smaller stage is home to chamber music recitals.
Götaplaten. Tel: (031) 726 53 10. www.gso.se

Lorensbergsteatern
This is Gothenburg's main location for theatrical performances, the majority being staged in Swedish.
Lorensbergsparken.
Tel: (031) 708 62 00.

Scandinavium
The huge arena, with a capacity for 14,000

people, is the city's main venue for big-name rock concerts. Past performers include Britney Spears and Bob Dylan. It's also the setting for sports events and musicals.
Vallhallagatan 1.
www.scandinavium.se

MALMÖ
Clubs and bars
Centileter & Gram
Probably the most popular bar in the city, on the main square. On summer evenings the crowd spills out onto the pavement to carry on drinking and socialising.
Stortorget 17.
Tel: (040) 12 18 12.

Mello Yello
Set in the picturesque courtyard area of Lilla Torg, the patio heaters placed around the pavement tables in summer ensure a warm atmosphere.
Lilla Torg 1.
Tel: (040) 30 45 25.

Slagthuset
Set in a former slaughterhouse, this is now the largest nightclub in Scandinavia. There is

also a theatre and conference hall on the site.
Jörgen Koksgatan 7a.
Tel: (040) 10 99 00.

Music and theatre
Jeriko
Swedish folk music, world music from Latin America and Africa, and traditional and modern jazz all feature prominently at the city's main music venue.
Kulturcentralen.

Konserthuset
The Malmö Symphony Orchestra performs more than 70 concerts a year, also welcoming international artists to its stage. The annual Teddy Bear concerts for children are popular.

Föreningsgatan.
Tel: (040) 630 45 00.

Malmö Opera and Music Theatre
The centre of all theatrical events in the city, this is the setting for opera, theatre and dance. There are also performances aimed especially at children.
Östra Rönneholmsvägen 20. Tel: (040) 20 85 00.
www.malmoopera.se

Skånes Dansteater
The finest contemporary dance company in Scandinavia has just celebrated its tenth anniversary.
Båghallarna, Östra Varvsgatan 13.
www.skanesdansteater.se

ICE GLOBE THEATRE, LAPLAND

It isn't just the main cities that offer entertainment spectacles. As part of the Ice Hotel complex (*see p178*), the Sami abode of Lapland in Sweden's far north sees a crude reconstruction of Shakespeare's Globe Theatre each year from December to mid-March, when freezing temperatures allow it. It is made entirely of ice. Beneath the polar night, and often with the added enchantment of the northern lights dancing overhead, watching a Sami production of *Hamlet* or *Macbeth* or classical opera is an unmissable experience. The audience sits on ice benches covered with reindeer skin while the actors perform on an ice stage under the stars. Even though you won't understand the Sami language, the whole atmosphere is unfailingly entrancing. Just don't forget to dress warmly.
Jukkasjärvi. www.icehotel.com

Children

Sweden is a wonderful destination for a family holiday, particularly the offshore islands with their abundance of sandy beaches and the opportunity to participate in gentle watersports. Even the cities gear many of their sights towards children, with interactive museum exhibits and open-air museums, often with children's petting zoos. Most hotels allow children under 12 to stay for free, and most sights offer reduced-price entry fees or family tickets.

According to European law, all children must now have their own passport. In addition, single parents may be required to show documentation that indicates permission from the absent parent for the child's travel or documentation proving sole parental responsibility. The Swedish Embassy in your country of residence will be able to offer more information.

Beaches

With its long coastline Sweden has more than enough beaches to satisfy children of any age and without the vast overcrowding that one usually finds in southern Europe. In addition the climate is warm and balmy, rather than sweltering, so it's safer for young skins. The waters too are calm and clean.

Museums

Like the rest of Scandinavia, Sweden loves its open-air museums and these can be a wonderful way to explain history to children – whether re-creations of the 19th century or the Viking era – by bringing it to life rather than through boring textbooks or relics. Many of these museums, such as Skansen in Stockholm (*see p39*), also have zoo areas where children can see animals native to the country up close.

Theme parks

Sweden was home to one of the world's finest children's writers, Astrid Lindgren. Several theme parks around the country – such as Junibacken in Stockholm (*see p38*) and Astrid Lindgrens Värld in Vimmerby (*see pp81–2*) – re-create the stories of Pippi Longstocking and her friends with life-size houses and actors dressed in the characters' costumes. Other theme parks are filled with amusement rides and live shows to entertain the whole family.

Ölands Djurpark

One of the country's best theme parks has plenty of amusement rides, including a roller coaster and a Ferris wheel, as well as a zoo, dinosaur park, circus acts and plenty of water rides to make a splash (*see p74*).

Skara Sommarland

This is the largest amusement park in Scandinavia. Rides include a themed roller coaster and a 70km/h (45mph) water chute. There's also a zoo, bumper cars and quad bikes, as well as a toddler's area. Family accommodation is also available at the park. Next door to the park is an area known as Fame World, with bungee jumps and paintballing for slightly older kids.

Skara. Tel: (46) 511 770 300. www.sommarland.se. Open: Jun daily 10am–5pm, July–mid-Aug daily 10am–7pm. Admission charge.

Safaris

To get close to nature and a truly unique experience head north to the Kiruna region where dog-sledging trips and elk safaris will delight children of all ages, as well as the adults. Tourist offices in the region will have information on all the different companies that organise these trips.

Kolmårdens Djurpark (Kolmården Safari Park)

For a safari of a more traditional nature, head to Kolmården where parents can drive through the park to encounter African beasts such as lions and leopards. There's also a children's park featuring domestic and farmyard animals, and an enchanting dolphinarium (*see pp68–9*).

Trampolining at Kungsträdgården

Sport and leisure

Swedes are as proud of their natural landscape as it is possible for a nation to be, and for this reason are fond of the great outdoor race, regularly taking to the water or the ski slopes for annual holidays or weekend breaks. There is something for everyone all year round, with snow and ice activities dominating the winter calendar, and the balmy coastline filled with sun-seekers in summer.

Canoeing and kayaking

Even novice canoeists can take to the calm waters of Sweden's inland lakes and canals to enjoy the scenery from the water. Those with more experience can also set off for the many coastal islands in sea kayaks. Various operators across the country hire out canoes for trips of varying lengths. There's even the possibility of building your own timber raft and floating along the Klarälven River (*see pp152–3*). *www.kanotguiden.com*

Cycling

The whole of Sweden is covered with marked cycle tracks and there can be few better ways to take in the landscape in spring and summer than from the seat of a bicycle, particularly on the many offshore islands. If you haven't brought your own bike there are numerous rental companies all over the country. Furthermore, particularly in the south, many of the paths are gentle, ambling routes, making them ideal for families. Mountain-biking enthusiasts should head for the Härjedalen region, which boasts more than 30 gentle peaks.

Fishing

Fishing is something of an obsession in Sweden, with its rivers and streams abundant with salmon, trout and many other fish. There are also some 200 species of saltwater fish to be found along the coast. Some of the best salmon fishing is to be found on Lake Vättern, the Mörrum River near Karlshamn and in the Emån River near Oskarshamn. No licence is required for hand-held equipment such as needed for rod fishing, but for net and sport fishing a permit (*Sveafiskekortet*) can be obtained from the Sveaskog institution. Several companies, such as **Fishing Sweden** (*www.fishing-sweden.com*), offer courses in fly fishing for beginners. In the north, in winter, ice fishing is a wonderfully novel experience. With lakes and rivers frozen over, anglers lie on their stomachs on a reindeer-skin rug, cut a hole in the ice and fish for Arctic char.

Sveafiskekortet. Tel: (46) 8 704 44 80.

Golf

There are more than 400 golf courses in Sweden, but you must have membership of a golf club in your home country in order to play. One of the prime areas for golf is the Skåne region in the south, with more than 70 courses, but there are also several around both Stockholm and Gothenburg.

www.golf-sweden.com

Hiking

Mountains, lakes, rivers and valleys all make for excellent hiking and walking possibilities. Maps of marked trails can be found in local tourist offices. For longer mountain hikes there are mountain lodges run by the voluntary STF association as well as simpler self-catering huts. The majority of the trails in the south are relaxing and require only a basic level of fitness, but those in the north are more demanding, and require both expertise and equipment. For both, however, it is important to wear decent walking boots and wear layers of clothing to cope with the changeable weather.

www.svenskaturistforeningen.se

Horse riding

Swedes are keen equestrians and it is easy to see why – Sweden offers a dramatic variety of terrain to the rider. Riders can choose between forests or beaches, guided tours or individual

Warm clothes are essential for ice fishing

outings. On the island of Gotland the Gotland pony is an indigenous breed that is ideal for children because of its gentle, steady gait. Icelandic ponies are also suitable for child riders.

Hunting

The elk hunting season is from August to February and some 100,000 are shot yearly in the dense forests which they inhabit. Tourists who wish to hunt in Sweden must join a hunting co-operative or book an excursion with a private landowner, pay an annual hunting conservation fee, have the correct level of insurance and take a shooting test arranged by the trip organisers. You will also have to hire a gun for the duration of the sport. Game hunting with tracker dogs is also available.

Skiing

Northern Sweden is the place for the best downhill skiing, the two major resorts being Åre (*see p135*) and Sälen (*see p138*). There are pistes to suit all levels. The added benefit is that the hordes of foreign tourists one finds crowding Switzerland, France and Austria are absent here. Riksgränsen is the most northerly resort in Europe and one of its unique charms is the opportunity to ski in summer under the midnight sun, wearing little more than shorts and a T-shirt, and with daylight continuing till 11pm.

Heli-skiing, where chartered helicopters take skiers to slopes

You need to have membership of a golf club in your home country in order to play golf

inaccessible any other way, is also popular. Swedes also take an almost spiritual attitude towards cross-country skiing, with its opportunity to glide across the crunchy snow, deep into the wilderness of pine and birch forests. Cross-country skiing is available all over the country, and not just the north, with a multitude of marked trails, many of which are floodlit at night.

Watersports

The southern coastline as well as the Stockholm archipelago are ideal for summer watersports such as windsurfing, waterskiing and swimming. The waters are calm and warm and many of the beaches sport a blue flag indicating safety and cleanliness. Boating of all levels is possible, from yachting to rowing, with more than 400 harbours in which to drop anchor.

White-water rafting

Raft trips follow an international grading system of levels I to VI, with I being suitable for a novice, and VI for experts who have rafted many times before. Rafting is possible in the north of Sweden in Kiruna, where the melted ice waters from the glaciers flow at breakneck speed.
www.kanotguiden.com

Winter sports

Speed-freaks will love the opportunity to race across the ice packs in snowmobiles over marked trails, but if you prefer someone else to do the driving head to Jukkasjärvi for a dog-sledding trip, where packs of yelping huskies pull you deep into the wilderness, offering one of the truest nature experiences in the world.

Even in towns and cities Swedes get their skates out in the beginning of November when ponds, lakes and streams ice over and turn into recreation centres. With more experienced skaters, trip skating, which covers long-distance routes over frozen rivers, is very popular.

Northern Sweden is the best place for downhill skiing

Food and drink

Sweden takes its cuisine and the quality of service very seriously and this becomes apparent from the very first meal you eat here. In the last few years Stockholm and Gothenburg have become gastronomic meccas, with several restaurateurs winning Michelin stars for their innovative use of the abundant local produce. Snacks are also an important aspect of the Swedish diet: hot-dog stands are a regular sight, and the tradition of an afternoon coffee with sweet pastry is still going strong.

WHAT TO EAT

Fish and seafood

With its extensive coastline and inland lakes, fish is unsurprisingly a staple of the Swedish diet. Salmon is abundant in the country's rivers and streams and is a major feature of most menus, served grilled, poached or fried. A popular starter or light lunch is *gravad lax*, in which raw salmon is marinated in sugar and dill, and served with a mustard sauce. Swedish oysters are considered a delicacy because of the cool waters of the Baltic in which they breed, and are often combined with lobster, prawns and mussels to form a seafood stew. Eel, trout, herring, fish roe, crayfish and crab are also regular features on the Swedish table.

Meat

Game is very popular in Sweden, and one of the more unique items on a meat menu is reindeer steak, a tender but strong-tasting cut that is usually grilled and served with a mushroom sauce.

Swedish meatballs (*köttbullar*) are something of a national dish, as can be seen by their presence on the Ikea menu all over the world. Pork is also popular, primarily in sausage form (*falukorv*) or in a yellow pea soup (*ärtsoppa*), and salted beef with turnips is another staple. Lingonberry jam often accompanies meat dishes to add a bit of lightness to otherwise hearty cooking.

Desserts

It's no secret that Swedes have a sweet tooth, and desserts (*efterrätt*) are a

COMMON FOODS

ägg	egg	**öl**	beer
bröt	bread	**ost**	cheese
fisk	fish	**potatis**	potatoes
forell	trout	**ris**	rice
glass	ice cream	**sill**	herring
kaffe	coffee	**skaldjur**	seafood
kött	meat	**smör**	butter
kyckling	chicken	**socker**	sugar
lamm	lamb	**soppa**	soup
mjöllk	milk	**te**	tea
nötkött	beef	**vin**	wine

major feature on any menu. Much use is made of native fruits, including the delicious cloudberries. Another speciality is rosehip soup, which is usually served as a cold dessert with vanilla ice cream. Pastries such as cinnamon buns and rich, calorie-high gateaux are also regulars on the menu.

Akvavit schnapps

SMÖRGÅSBORD

The most famous food to come out of Sweden is its own version of tapas or mezze. The *smörgåsbord* – which literally translates as 'sandwich table' – is a buffet of small dishes, usually cold, which diners can pick and choose from indefinitely for a fixed price. The most common feature is herring (sill), which is served pickled, fried, smoked or marinated in mustard. Other ingredients include anchovies, potatoes, eel, smoked salmon and fish roe, as well as accompaniments such as sour cream. At Christmas time the *smörgåsbord* is known as *Julbord* ('yule table'), which includes seasonal dishes such as baked ham served with bread and mustard.

Vegetarians

Unless you are prepared to eat fish or seafood, vegetarian options are fairly limited in Sweden and are largely restricted to bland salads, omelettes and cheese, although the larger cities will have ethnic restaurants such as Indian and Chinese where vegetarian choices will be much more widespread.

WHAT TO DRINK

Coffee could almost be called the national drink in Sweden, with one of the highest consumptions in the world. Milk, too, is drunk on a daily basis. Wine features on restaurant menus but is all imported so prices are high. Most Swedes stick to beer or *Akvavit* schnapps, a distilled drink flavoured with herbs, for their alcoholic choices. At Christmas, *glögg* (mulled wine) and *julmust*, a non-alcoholic drink made from hops and spices, are drunk.

WHERE TO EAT

The choice of restaurants is high all over Sweden, with the people taking both food and socialising very seriously. Traditional Swedish food can be found in even the smallest villages, and in the cities there are, of course, plenty of options for ethnic dining. The Swedes are particularly fond of Italian and Asian cuisines.

★	Less than 275 Kr
★★	275–450 Kr
★★★	450–650 Kr
★★★★	Over 650 Kr

Stockholm

Berns ★★

This is certainly the most elegant and spectacular dining setting in Stockholm, with the Baroque gilded dining room renovated by Sir Terence Conran. The menu is largely international, but there are Swedish specialities such as a traditional herring plate for starter and roasted venison or baked salmon as a main course.
Berzelii Park 9.
Tel: (08) 566 325 15.

Smak på Restaurangen™ ★★

Run by the same chef as Fredsgatan 12, the emphasis here is on the traditional *smörgåsbord* idea of several small dishes rather than the classic three courses, each one created on the premise of taste, such as a specific herb or spice.
Oxtorgsgatan 14.
Tel: (08) 2 209 52.

Victoria ★★

On the buzzing stretch of the city that is Kungsträdgården (*see pp52–3*), Victoria offers a menu of Swedish classics such as meatballs and shrimp salad with a lively atmosphere. Most nights in summer there is some form of entertainment; sit at the pavement tables for a quieter atmosphere.
Kungsträdgården.
Tel: (08) 218 600.

Den Gyldene Freden ★★★

The best restaurant in the Old Town is consistently popular, so it's essential to book ahead. The décor is intimate, lit with candles, and the menu focuses on fish – turbot and smelt are regular features. There is both a set menu and à la carte.
Österlånggatan.
Tel: (08) 249 760.

Mårten Trotzig ★★★

Evocatively set opposite the tiniest alleyway in the Old Town, of the same name, this is a highly popular restaurant serving Swedish classic dishes such as reindeer in a port sauce and salmon baked with saffron and fennel. The décor is modern and elegant.
Västerlånggatan 79.
Tel: (08) 442 25 30.

The sophisticated Berns restaurant in Stockholm

Classic Swedish fare is on the menu at Victoria

Sturehof ★★★

Run by one of the country's most prolific restaurateurs, P G Nilsson, this vast restaurant is open every day of the year until 1am. The menu incorporates French bistro classics, but Swedish specialities include fried pike served with beetroot.
Stureplan 2.
Tel: (08) 4 40 5730.

Fredsgatan 12 ★★★★

Sweden's most famous chef, Melker Andersson, runs his Michelin-starred waterfront flagship restaurant with style and precision. Among the mouthwatering dishes on offer are seared tuna tossed with olives, anchovies and cucumber, truffle tortellini, roe deer steak with apple and celery, and a delectable chocolate plate served with exotic fruits.
Fredsgatan 12.
Tel: (08) 2 480 52.

Gothenburg

Barken Viking ★★★

In summer this historic boat serves an international and Swedish menu on the deck, offering wonderful waterside views (*see pp56–7*).
Gullbergskajen.
Tel: (031) 6 358 00.

Basement ★★★

The emphasis here is on Swedish cuisine, and there's a tasting menu allowing you to sample many smaller dishes.
Götabergsgatan 28.
Tel: (031) 282 729.

Fiskekrogen ★★★

Renowned as one of the city's finest fish restaurants, with grilled turbot served with caviar among the specialities.
Lilla Torget 1.
Tel: (031) 101 005.

Fond ★★★

This Michelin-starred restaurant is renowned for its traditional food with a modern twist, such as cod loin baked in brown butter.
Götaplatsen.
Tel: (031) 8 125 80.

28+ ★★★

A luxurious institution in Gothenburg, rated as much for its elegant food as for its extensive wine cellar.
Götabergsgatan 28.
Tel: (031) 202 161.

Sjömagasinet ★★★★

Another Michelin-starred offering, and with its position beside the port it's not surprising that the fish and seafood are the highlights of the menu. Try the crayfish with dill, followed by halibut in a lime sauce, finished off with a wonderful platter of local cheese served with marmalade.
Adolf Edelsvärds gata 5.
Tel: (031) 775 5920.

Accommodation

Accommodation in Sweden is of an extremely high standard, and en-suite facilities and cleanliness are features even at the lowest end of the scale. The cities of Stockholm and Gothenburg feature not only luxury chain hotels, but also elegant boutique hotels where the focus is on personal service and elegant surroundings. In rural areas authentic wooden cottages and family-run guesthouses are the best places to get a feel of local life.

TYPES OF ACCOMMODATION
Hotels

In all of Sweden's cities the Scandinavian chains Radisson SAS, Scandic Rica and Choice will have at least one hotel, as well as international chains such as Ramada and Best Western. As both Stockholm and Gothenburg make ideal weekend destinations, many hotels offer favourable weekend packages to make up for the lack of their usual weekly business clientele. There are three official hotel categories in Sweden: 'hotel' implies there is an on-site restaurant, 'hotel Garni' are 4-star hotels and under, but only serve breakfast, while 'hotel S' indicates a seasonal hotel. Both Stockholm and Gothenburg are big conference cities, so make sure you book ahead in summer.

Guesthouses and bed & breakfasts

This is a cheaper option in major towns and often the only choice in the rural areas. Many farmhouses rent out rooms on a bed & breakfast basis; look out for the word *rum*, which indicates availability. Most offer outdoor activities.

Hostels

There are more than 450 youth hostels (*vandrarhem*) in Sweden, which, despite their name, do not have any age

Gothia Towers Hotel

restrictions for guests, although you must be a member of the International Youth Hostel Association or one of its affiliates. Accommodation varies between double, triple, family and dormitory-style rooms, and free self-catering facilities are included. In the summer season it's usually advisable to book in advance.
www.stfturist.se

Camping and cottages

The 'every man's right' to all land in Sweden means that camping is one of the easiest options for those who like to stay close to nature. The only restrictions are that campers should not be within sight of houses or on private land. However, there are also official campsites offering mod cons such as washrooms and cooking facilities for a more comfortable stay. If you want a firmer roof over your head, many campsites also rent out cottages with self-catering facilities. Waterfront cabins are also a popular and very traditional accommodation option.
www.camping.se

Castles and manor houses

More than 40 stately homes and manor houses with a fascinating historic past have now been converted into hotel accommodation in the heart of the countryside, making for a wonderfully evocative and romantic stay. Excellent cuisine combined with ornate architecture and furnishings all add to the experience.
www.countrysidehotels.se

Summerhouse by a lake

Accommodation

WHERE TO STAY

The star ratings indicate the average cost of accommodation for a double room per night.

★	Less than 700 Kr
★★	700–1,500 Kr
★★★	1,500–2,000 Kr
★★★★	More than 2,000 Kr

Stockholm

AF Chapman ★

Moored on the island of Skeppsholmen, this 100-year-old boat is now a youth hostel with bunk beds in the former cabins.
Flaggmansvägen 8.
Tel: (46) 8 463 22 66.

Mälardrottningen Hotel ★★

The former yacht of millionaire Barbara Hutton is now a unique hotel, preserving the mahogany and brass furnishings from its seafaring days, while the former cabins offer all the mod cons one would expect from a 21st-century hotel. There are great views of the Gamla Stan area.
Riddarholmen.
Tel: (46) 8 545 187 80.

August Strindberg Hotel ★★★

This quiet hotel, which is named after Sweden's national playwright and includes a garden where breakfast can be eaten in summer, offers elegantly designed rooms at a good price for such a central location.
Tegnergatan 38.
Tel: (46) 8 32 50 06.

Best Western Hotel Terminus ★★★

Part of the international chain, this is a very central location near Kungsträdgården and shops and restaurants. The rooms are simple but stylish and there's a nice bar and bistro on the ground floor.
Vasagatan 20.
Tel: (46) 8 440 1670.

Colonial Hotel ★★★

An extremely central position, moments from the Central Station, but at very competitive prices. Not all rooms are en-suite, so make sure you request a bathroom when booking if so desired.
Västmannagatan 13.
Tel: (46) 8 217 630.

Berns Hotel ★★★★

This is one of the finest boutique hotels in the city, with 65 rooms where every attention to detail has been paid. Pale wood and white linen are perfectly offset by other stylish furnishings. In addition, the hotel also boasts one of the most elegant restaurants in town. A favourite with celebrities and politicians.
Näckströmsgatan 8.
Tel: (46) 8 566 322 00.

THE ICE HOTEL

Every winter between October and April, in the town of Jukkasjärvi, a hotel is built entirely of ice and snow, with 60 rooms, an ice chandelier and a world-famous vodka bar where drinks are served in glasses carved from ice. Guests are equipped with thermal sleeping bags and reindeer skins to keep them warm, and wake up to a cup of hot lingonberry juice. The hotel also organises activities such as dog-sledging and elk safaris. It all comes at a price, but this must surely be one of the most unusual accommodation options in the world.
Tel: (46) 980 668 00.
www.icehotel.com

Grand Hôtel Stockholm ★★★★

Probably the best address in town – as any guest will realise the minute they see its harbourside location and the sumptuous foyer, complete with columns and chandeliers. Don't expect modern minimalism here – even the rooms are decked out as if they were royal Baroque apartments. Of course, it comes at a price, but if money is no object or for a special occasion there can be no better place.
Södra Blasieholmshamnen 8. Tel: (46) 8 679 35 00.

Hotel Diplomat ★★★★

With the arguable exception of the Grand, this is Stockholm's premier place to stay. Set in a distinctive 1920s building, rooms have been decorated in modern style without losing any of their historic character, while the T/Bar is the height of trendy design.
Strandvägen 7c. Tel: (46) 8 459 68 00.

Hotel Rival ★★★★

This boutique hotel on the trendy island of Södermalm is owned by former ABBA band member Benny Andersson. The 99 rooms are all beautifully designed, with Egyptian cotton sheets, plasma-screen TVs and high-tech Internet equipment. There's also a very popular bar and bistro, and the hotel even has its own cinema.
Mariatorget 3. Tel: (46) 8 545 789 00.

Gothenburg
Hotel Flora ★

The cheapest place to stay in central Gothenburg, this family-run hotel is comfortable, friendly and close to the shopping area of Avenyn.
Grönsakstorget 2. Tel: (46) 31 13 86 16.

Avalon Hotel ★★

Gothenburg's newest boutique hotel opened in 2007 in the heart of the city. The décor is classic Scandinavian with pale wood and cutting-edge design. The penthouse suite even has its own swimming pool.
Kungstorget 9. Tel: (46) 31 751 02 00.

Hôtel Eggers ★★★

One of the oldest hotels in Sweden and set in a listed building, the Eggers has retained its historic style with lavish furnishings and chandeliers, but has equipped its rooms with modern amenities.
Drottningtorget. Tel: (46) 31 333 44 40.

Elite Plaza Hotel ★★★★

The most luxurious place to stay in the city, set within a 19th-century building renovated recently but preserving its original mosaic floors and stucco details. Some of the rooms have four-poster beds, while the restaurant is set in an outdoor courtyard covered by a 20m (66ft) high glass roof.
Västra Hamngatan 3. Tel: (46) 31 720 40 00.

Practical guide

Arriving

Citizens of the UK, USA, Australia, Canada, New Zealand and Ireland require a valid passport for a stay of less than three months. Citizens of all other nations should check with the Swedish embassy about entry requirements.

By air

Stockholm has three international airports, Arlanda, Skavsta and Bromma, with the main traffic arriving and departing from Arlanda. There are also international airports at Gothenburg and Malmö. The main international traffic in and out of Sweden is operated by SAS (Scandinavian Airlines), British Airways and Finnair. For no-frills travel, Ryanair operates budget flights to Stockholm (Skavsta) and Gothenburg from London Stansted.

By bus

Express coaches operate between Norway and Sweden, in particular between Stockholm, Gothenburg and Oslo. Journey times can be long (seven hours between the two capitals) but the buses are comfortable with toilet facilities and the prices are lower than air and train travel (*www.resplus.se*).

By car

Motorists can drive from Denmark to Sweden over the Öresund Bridge, or take one of the many car ferries that ply the route daily. There are also good motorway routes between Norway, Sweden and Finland and border crossings are straightforward – you may not even have to show your passport although you should have it handy.

By sea

DFDS (*www.dfdsseaways.se*) operates a ferry service between Harwich in England and Esbjerg in Denmark, from where it is possible to reach Sweden by train. **Scandlines** (*www.scandlines.se*) operates a ferry service between Helnsingør in Denmark and Helsingborg. Most ferries from Stockholm, such as **Viking Line** (*www.vikingline.se*), cover the Baltic Sea route between Sweden, Finland and Tallinn in Estonia.

By train

There is a daily train service between Stockholm and Oslo, while the Öresund Bridge (*see p81*) ensures that there are fast rail connections between Copenhagen and Malmö with onward routes to Stockholm and Gothenburg. For up-to-date details of rail services, consult the *Thomas Cook European Rail Timetable*, which is published monthly (*see p188*).

Climate

The best time to visit Sweden is between May and August, when the weather is considerably warmer, but a

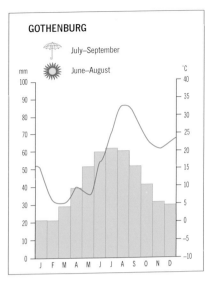

GOTHENBURG

July–September

June–August

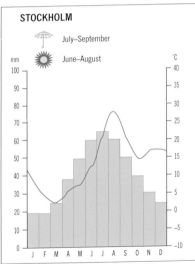

STOCKHOLM

July–September

June–August

WEATHER CONVERSION CHART

25.4mm = 1 inch

°F = 1.8 × °C + 32

Practical guide

CONVERSION TABLE

FROM	TO	MULTIPLY BY
Inches	Centimetres	2.54
Feet	Metres	0.3048
Yards	Metres	0.9144
Miles	Kilometres	1.6090
Acres	Hectares	0.4047
Gallons	Litres	4.5460
Ounces	Grams	28.35
Pounds	Grams	453.6
Pounds	Kilograms	0.4536
Tons	Tonnes	1.0160

To convert back, for example from centimetres to inches, divide by the number in the third column.

MEN'S SUITS

UK	36	38	40	42	44	46	48
Rest of Europe	46	48	50	52	54	56	58
USA	36	38	40	42	44	46	48

DRESS SIZES

UK	8	10	12	14	16	18
France	36	38	40	42	44	46
Italy	38	40	42	44	46	48
Rest of Europe	34	36	38	40	42	44
USA	6	8	10	12	14	16

MEN'S SHIRTS

UK	14	14.5	15	15.5	16	16.5	17
Rest of Europe	36	37	38	39/40	41	42	43
USA	14	14.5	15	15.5	16	16.5	17

MEN'S SHOES

UK	7	7.5	8.5	9.5	10.5	11
Rest of Europe	41	42	43	44	45	46
USA	8	8.5	9.5	10.5	11.5	12

WOMEN'S SHOES

UK	4.5	5	5.5	6	6.5	7
Rest of Europe	38	38	39	39	40	41
USA	6	6.5	7	7.5	8	8.5

Stockholm's Central Station

warm fleece or jacket as well as an umbrella should always be part of your packing regime.

Crime and safety

Sweden is probably one of the safest countries in the world in terms of crime, but common-sense attitudes should still prevail, such as leaving valuables in the hotel safe and out of sight when leaving a parked car. Pickpockets do operate, particularly around stations in the main cities and within large crowds during summer festivals, so keep an eye on your belongings. Report any theft to the police – most policemen in Sweden speak fluent English.

Customs regulations

Visitors from within the EU may import 110 litres of beer, 10 litres of spirits and 90 litres of wine. For those visiting from outside the EU, however, imports are limited to one litre of spirits, two litres of wine and beer valued at less that 1,700 Kr. All visitors must be 20 or over to import alcohol. Visitors may also import 400 cigarettes.

Driving
Car hire

All the major car-hire firms such as Avis, Budget, Hertz and Europcar have offices at Sweden's international and domestic airports and in major cities. Car hire, however, is expensive, so it might be worth making use of the far cheaper weekend deals, hiring a vehicle from Friday afternoon until Monday morning, and look out for restrictions on mileage if you're planning to travel long distances.

Emergency

For emergency breakdown assistance, call *020 91 00 40*. Sweden also has two companies – **Assistancekåren** (*tel: 020 912 912*) and **Falck** (*tel: 020 38 38 38*) – that will come to your roadside aid if you organise an agreement between them and your automobile organisation or insurance company prior to your trip. Emergency telephones can be found along motorways.

Insurance

Third-party insurance is compulsory and a Green Card is recommended.

Petrol

Petrol is available in leaded and unleaded form. Petrol stations in cities and larger towns are abundant, usually self-service and open seven days a week, and some are open 24 hours. In rural areas, however, they may be sparser and it's essential to check opening times, as many close as early as 6pm and for the entire weekend. Diesel is almost essential in the north in winter because it doesn't freeze.

Roads

The roads in Sweden are of a very high standard and are divided into three categories: motorway, national road and county road. The large majority of road signs in Sweden use international highway symbols. Unlike many of its European counterparts, there are no toll roads in the country apart from the Öresund Bridge. It is obligatory to drive with dipped headlights on, 24 hours a day, and to wear both front and rear seat belts. Children under seven should be seated in special baby or child seats. If driving in snowy conditions, tyre chains or studded tyres should be attached to the wheels. Cars drive on the right-hand side of the road.

Speed limits

The speed limit in towns and cities is 50km/h (31mph), on open roads 70km/h (43mph), and on motorways 110km/h (68mph). Limits are strictly enforced and speeding fines are very high.

Electricity

Sweden uses 220 volts and two-pin European plugs.

Embassies and consulates

Australia *Sergels Torg 12, 11th floor, Stockholm. Tel: (46) 8 613 29 00.*
Canada *Tegelbacken 4, 7th floor, Stockholm. Tel: (46) 8 453 3000.*
Ireland
Stockholm: *Ostermalmsgatan 97. Tel: (46) 8 661 8005.*
Gothenburg: *Massans Gata 18. Tel: (46) 31 836 930.*
UK
Stockholm: *Skarpögatan 6–8. Tel: (46) 705 16 00 33.*
Gothenburg: *Sextantgatan 14. Tel: (031) 696 453.*
USA *Dag Hammarskjölds Väg 31, Stockholm. Tel: (46) 8 783 5300.*

Emergency telephone numbers

Police, fire and ambulance, *tel: 112.*

Health and insurance

There are no vaccinations required to visit Sweden, although inoculation against tetanus is always advisable. Tap water is safe to drink all over the country. All doctors, hospital staff, dentists and pharmacists have a good command of English. Healthcare is inexpensive for European citizens provided they are carrying a European Health Insurance Card, available online at *www.ehic.org.uk*, by phoning *0845 6062030* or from post offices. For minor ailments, pharmacists (*apotek*), indicated by a green cross or an *a* above their door, can be found in all towns and cities. If visiting mountain, lake or canal regions in summer take a good insect repellent as midges and non-malarial mosquitoes are major nuisances. If you are bitten badly, a pharmacist will be able to supply a non-prescriptive antihistamine cream. Around the islands there is also the risk of ticks, which need to be removed from the skin in their entirety with tweezers. Note that some medicines, such as codeine, which are available over the counter in other countries, require a prescription here.

Internet

Internet facilities are easy to come by, including in designated cafés and at stations and libraries. Most high-range hotels now include Internet facilities, either in individual rooms or in public areas near the reception.

Media

In large cities such as Stockholm and Gothenburg, the major British newspapers can usually be found, but may be one day old. American magazines such as *Time* and *The Economist* are also available, as is the *International Herald Tribune*. The leading Swedish papers are *Aftenbladet* and *Svenska Dagbladet*. The main Swedish television channels are SVT1, SVT2, TV3 and TV4, but British and American imports are presented in their original language with Swedish subtitles. Most high-end hotels have cable TV with English-speaking channels such as CNN and the BBC.

Money matters
Currency

The Swedish currency is the krona (SEK or Kr). One krona is made up of 100 öre. Coins come in the following denominations: 50 öre and 1, 5 and 10 Kr. Krona notes come in denominations of 20, 50, 100, 500 and 1,000.

Exchange

Most major towns and cities have ATMs that accept certain foreign credit and debit cards, although you may be charged for the transaction, depending on the card.

Traveller's cheques in major currencies can be exchanged at banks and post offices.

Credit cards

All the major credit cards – Visa, MasterCard, Eurocard and Diners Club – are readily accepted across Sweden, except perhaps in the smallest shops. American Express users, however, may encounter problems as the Swedes do not willingly accept the high rates enforced on the retailer.

National holidays

1 January New Year's Day
6 January Epiphany
March–April Easter Friday to Easter Monday
Sixth Thursday after Easter Ascension Day
1 May Labour Day
6 June National Day
22–23 June Midsummer

Language

Most Swedes speak fluent or at least competent English, but it is always useful to learn a few local phrases. There are 29 letters in the Swedish alphabet, which includes all the letters of the Latin alphabet as well as ä, å and ö.

TIME		NUMBERS	
Today	Idag	**1**	ett
Yesterday	Igår	**2**	två
Tomorrow	I morgon	**3**	tre
What is the time?	Vad time er den?	**4**	fyre
		5	fem
DAYS OF THE WEEK		**6**	sex
Monday	Måndag	**7**	sju
Tuesday	Tisdag	**8**	åtta
Wednesday	Onsdag	**9**	nio
Thursday	Torsdag	**10**	tio
Friday	Fredag	**20**	tjugo
Saturday	Lördag	**100**	hundra
Sunday	Söndag	**1000**	tusen

EVERYDAY EXPRESSIONS		PRONUNCIATION	
Yes	Ja	å	as the o in 'sword'
No	Nej	ä	as the ai in 'flair'
There is	Där er	ö	as the u in 'fur'
There is not	Där er inte		
I want	Jag skulle vilja	**GREETINGS AND COURTESIES**	
How much?	Hur mycket?	**Hello**	Hej
Expensive	Dyr	**Goodbye**	Hej då
Cheap	Billig	**Good morning**	Godmorgon
Money	Pengar	**Good evening**	Godafton
Toilet	Toalett	**Good night**	God natt
Men's toilet	Herr	**Please**	Varsågod
Women's toilet	Damer	**Thank you**	Tack
		Excuse me	Ursäkta

3 Nov All Saints' Day
24 December Christmas Eve
25 December Christmas Day
26 December Boxing Day
31 December New Year's Eve

Opening hours

Shops are usually open from Monday to Friday 9.30am–6pm, and until 2 or 4pm on Saturday. Most banks are open from Monday to Friday 10am–3pm (until 4pm on Thursday). Many museums are closed on Mondays, and a large majority of them close their doors during the winter months or reduce their operating times.

Organised tours

Tourist offices all over the country will be happy to organise specialised tours for you, be it a wildlife safari, a marked hike, or a city tour.

Pharmacies

Pharmacies (*apotek*) are open during business hours, and are highly qualified in diagnosing and treating minor ailments, and all pharmacists are required to be fluent in English. If you need a pharmacist outside business hours there will be a sign in the window indicating the nearest all-night pharmacy.

Police

The Swedish police (*polisen*) service is divided into 21 districts, but they all come under the jurisdiction of the National Police Board. They can be identified by the royal coat of arms on their uniforms and should be consulted immediately if you are a victim of any crime.

Post offices

Sweden has post offices (*postkontor*) in all towns and cities. These can be identified by a blue and yellow sign depicting a crown and a trumpet. Poste restante services are available. Post boxes can be found in the street, and are coloured yellow for national and international mail and blue for local mail. Stamps can be bought at post offices as well as at newspaper stands and anywhere that you can buy postcards.

Public transport

By air

Sweden has 47 airports that handle domestic flights, which makes negotiating the long distances involved quite easy. **SAS** (*www.sas.no*), **Skyways** (*www.skyways.se*) and **Malmö Aviation** (*www.malmoaviation.se*) service a number of domestic destinations. Tickets can be bought online and picked up at the relevant airport, but local travel agents will also book flights for you. For most domestic flights, check-in is no later than 15 minutes before departure.

By bus

Information about the country's express and local bus networks can be found at **Samtrafiken** (*www.resplus.se*). Tickets for most express buses must be

Stockholm Metro

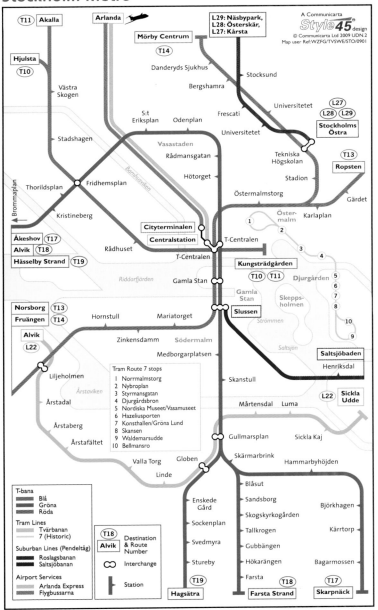

A Communicarta
Style45 design
© Communicarta Ltd 2009 UDN.2
Map user Ref:WZFG/TVSWE/STO/0901

T11 Akalla

Arlanda

L29: Näsbypark,
L28: Österskär,
L27: Kårsta

Mörby Centrum

T14

Hjulsta
T10

Danderyds Sjukhus

Stocksund

Västra
Skogen

Bergshamra

Universitetet L27
L28 L29
Stockholms
Östra

S:t
Eriksplan Odenplan

Frescati

Stadshagen

Vasastaden

Universitetet

Rådmansgatan

Tekniska
Högskolan T13
Ropsten

Hötorget

Stadion

Thorildsplan Fridhemsplan

Östermalmstorg

Gärdet

Kristineberg

Öster-
malm Karlaplan

Åkeshov T17
Alvik T18
Hässelby Strand T19

Rådhuset

Cityterminalen

Centralstation T-Centralen

1
2

T-Centralen

3
4

Kungsträdgården

Riddarfjärden Gamla Stan

T10 T11 Djurgården

5
6

Gamla
Stan

Skepps-
holmen

7
8

Norsborg T13
Fruängen T14

Hornstull Mariatorget

Slussen

Strömmen

10

9

Alvik
L22

Zinkensdamm Södermalm

Saltsjön

Saltsjöbaden

Medborgarplatsen

Henriksdal

Liljeholmen

Tram Route 7 stops
1 Norrmalmstorg
2 Nybroplan
3 Styrmansgatan
4 Djurgårdsbron
5 Nordiska Museet/Vasamuseet
6 Hazeliusporten
7 Konsthallen/Gröna Lund
8 Skansen
9 Waldemarsudde
10 Bellmansro

Skanstull

Årstaviken

Mårtensdal Luma

L22 Sickla
Udde

Årstadal

Årstaberg

Gullmarsplan Sickla Kaj

Årstafältet

Valla Torg

Globen

Skärmarbrink

Hammarbyhöjden

Linde

Blåsut

T-bana
Blå
Gröna
Röda

Tram Lines
Tvärbanan
7 (Historic)

Suburban Lines (Pendeltåg)
Roslagsbanan
Saltsjöbanan

Airport Services
Arlanda Express
Flygbussarna

T18
Alvik
Destination
& Route
Number

CO Interchange

Station

Enskede
Gård

Sockenplan

Svedmyra

Stureby

T19
Hagsätra

Sandsborg

Skogskyrkogården

Tallkrogen

Gubbängen

Hökarängen

Farsta

T18
Farsta Strand

Björkhagen

Kärrtorp

Bagarmossen

T17
Skarpnäck

bought in advance, but on **Swebus** routes (*www.swebusexpress.se*) tickets can be bought on board.

By ferry

Passenger ferries ply Sweden's long coastline throughout the summer to the various islands, including Gotland and Öland, and a passenger cruise travels the picturesque Göta Canal. If you're planning to visit several islands it is worth buying a ferry pass (*båtluffarkortet*) for unlimited travel over 16 days.

By metro

Stockholm's metro system is known as the Tunnelbana (or T-Bana) and consists of three lines covering most of the city.

By taxi

The easiest way to get a taxi in the cities is at a taxi rank, although you are allowed to hail one in the street if the cab's light is illuminated. In Stockholm you can call a cab on *30 00 00*. Taxi fares are up to the discretion of each taxi company so it is advisable to check the fare before starting the journey. Airport taxis have standardised fares.

By train

The **SJ** (Swedish State Railway) network (*www.sj.se*), including the X2000 high-speed services, covers a large part of the country. Tickets can be bought in advance or on the train, but the latter incurs higher prices. Overnight trains for longer journeys offer six-berth, three-berth or private berth accommodation.

Thomas Cook Timetable

For details and times of train, ferry and long-distance bus services consult the *Thomas Cook European Rail Timetable*, which can be bought online at *www.thomascookpublishing.com*, from branches of Thomas Cook in the UK or by phoning *tel: 01733 416477.*

Smoking

Since 2005 smoking has been banned in all public places. Smoking is permitted at outside tables of bars and restaurants.

Student travel

Students should carry an International Student Identity Card (ISIC), which will entitle them to valuable discounts on admission fees to sights, as well as on ferries and public transport.

Sustainable tourism

Thomas Cook is a strong advocate of ethical and fairly traded tourism and believes that the travel experience should be as good for the places visited as it is for the people that visit them. That's why we're a firm supporter of The Travel Foundation, a charity that develops solutions to help improve and protect holiday destinations, their environment, traditions and culture. To find out what you can do to make a positive difference to the places you travel to and the people who live there, please visit *www.thetravelfoundation.org.uk*

Taxes

All non-Scandinavian residents are entitled to claim back between 15 to 18 per cent of the tax paid on purchases above 200 Kr at shops that display a 'tax-free goods' sign. You must present your passport and ask for a tax-free shopping form. The form should be handed in to the Tax Free counter at your point of departure and a refund in krona will be handed to you.

Telephones

There are both card and credit-card public phone boxes in public areas and at post offices. Phonecards can be bought at post offices and kiosks (*pressbyrån*). To call abroad from Sweden, dial *00* then the appropriate country code. The country code for Sweden is *46*. For directory enquiries dial *118 118*. Mobile phone coverage, particularly in the south of the country, is very good.

Here are the main country codes, should you want to make an international call from Sweden.

Australia *00 61*
Ireland *00 353*
New Zealand *00 64*
UK *00 44*
USA and Canada *00 1*

Time

Sweden's time zone is GMT + one hour. The UK and Ireland are one hour behind, Australia and New Zealand are nine hours ahead, and the USA and Canada are six hours behind on the east coast, and nine hours behind on the west coast.

Tipping

Service charges are included in restaurant bills but it is still customary to add an extra 10 per cent. Taxi drivers also generally expect a small tip.

Tourist offices

Australia *5 Turrana Street, Yarralumla, ACT 2600. Tel: (00 61) 2 6270 2700.*
Canada *377 Dalhousie Street, Ottawa, ON K1N 9N8. Tel: (00 1) 613 244 8200.*
Ireland *13–17 Dawson Street, Dublin 2. Tel: (00 353) 1 671 58 22.*
UK *Sweden House, 5 Upper Montagu Street, London W1G 2AG. Tel: (020) 7870 5604.*
USA *655 Third Avenue, Suite 1810, New York NY 10017-5617. Tel: (00 1) 212 949 2333.*

Travellers with disabilities

Sweden is very well equipped for travellers with disabilities. **RADAR** (*www.radar.org.uk*) is a UK-based organisation that sells packs for a nominal fee detailing advice for travellers with disabilities abroad, while the Sweden-specific **De Handikappades Riksförbund** (*www.dhr.se*) also offers valuable advice.

The *Sankt Erik*, a museum ship in Stockholm

Index

Acknowledgements

Thomas Cook Publishing wishes to thank ALEX KOUPRIANOFF, to whom the copyright belongs, for the photographs in this book (except for the following images):

DREAMSTIME Sokolovsky 1
HENRIK REINHOLDSON 53
FLICKR jimmyroq 64
IMAGE BANK SWEDEN: Alex Brandell/Malmö Turism 170; Bitte Sturesson 83; Bo Kågerud/Svenska Mässan 176; Henry B. Goodwin/The Royal Library 24; Marie Birkl/Norrlandia 134; Patrick Trägårdh 11, 143, 164; Peter Grant 104, 108, 150, 151, 171; Håkan Sandbring/Positlõn Skåne/Sydpol.Com 76, 103; S Mezzanotte/Stockholm Visitors Board 163; Bo Lind/Swedish Travel And Tourism Council 169, 177; Wolfgang Greiner 146, 147, 154
ISTOCKPHOTO Jon Jakob 80; Lord Runar 84; alicat 124
JACQUELINE FRYD 6, 36, 45, 46, 48, 59, 60, 65, 68, 71, 87, 90, 101, 112, 116, 117a, 118, 119, 122, 129, 133, 173
KLAUS FUISTING 121
PATRICK STRANG 102
RAGUNDADALEN TOURISM 141
ROBIN GAULDIE/SARGASSO MEDIA LTD 5, 10, 15, 17, 21, 23, 31, 35, 37, 38, 41, 42, 43, 161, 167, 174, 175, 182, 189
THOMAS COOK 29
WIKIMEDIA COMMONS 16, 50 (Pellaj), 110 (Artifex), 137
WORLD PICTURES/ PHOTOSHOT 56

The photographer also thanks the SWEDISH EMBASSY OF BRUSSELS for providing the image on page 67.

FOR CAMBRIDGE PUBLISHING MANAGEMENT LIMITED:
Project editor: Frances Darby
Typesetter: Donna Pedley
Proofreader: Nick Newton
Indexer: Karolin Thomas

SEND YOUR THOUGHTS TO
BOOKS@THOMASCOOK.COM

We're committed to providing the very best up-to-date information in our travel guides and constantly strive to make them as useful as they can be. You can help us to improve future editions by letting us have your feedback. If you've made a wonderful discovery on your travels that we don't already feature, if you'd like to inform us about recent changes to anything that we do include, or if you simply want to let us know your thoughts about this guidebook and how we can make it even better – we'd love to hear from you.

Send us ideas, discoveries and recommendations today and then look out for your valuable input in the next edition of this title.

Emails to the above address, or letters to traveller guides Series Editor, Thomas Cook Publishing, PO Box 227, Coningsby Road, Peterborough PE3 8SB, UK.

Please don't forget to let us know which title your feedback refers to!